ReThink

life

How to Be Different from the Norm

Rodney and Michelle Gage

CROSSBOOKS
PUBLISHING

CrossBooks™
A Division of LifeWay
1663 Liberty Drive
Bloomington, IN 47403
www.crossbooks.com
Phone: 1-866-879-0502

Unless otherwise indicated, all Scripture quotations are taken from the Holy Bible, New Living
Translation, copyright © 1996, 2004, 2007 by Tyndale House Foundation. Used by permission
of Tyndale House Publishers, Inc., Carol Stream, Illinois 60188. All rights reserved.

Scripture quotations marked NIV are taken from The Holy Bible, New International Version®
NIV®. Copyright © 1973, 1978, 1984, 2011 by Biblica, Inc.™ Used by permission. All rights
reserved.

Scripture taken from GOD'S WORD®, © 1995 God's Word to the Nations. Used by permission
of Baker Publishing Group.

Scripture taken from The Message. Copyright © 1993, 1994, 1995, 1996, 2000, 2001, 2002.
Used by permission of NavPress Publishing Group.

Contemporary English Version® . Copyright © 1995 American Bible Society. All rights reserved.

Scripture quotations are from Revised Standard Version of the Bible. Copyright © 1946, 1952,
and 1971 National Council of the Churches of Christ in the United States of America. Used by
permission. All rights reserved.

Note: To protect the anonymity of some of the people in the stories, names and details have been
changed.

First published by CrossBooks 06/08/2012

ISBN: 978-1-4627-1441-4 (sc)
ISBN: 978-1-4627-1442-1 (e)

Library of Congress Control Number: 2012904007

Printed in the United States of America

This book is printed on acid-free paper.

Any people depicted in stock imagery provided by Thinkstock are models,
and such images are being used for illustrative purposes only.

Certain stock imagery © Thinkstock.

CONTENTS

Acknowledgments v

Preface vii

Chapter 1   Why ReThink Life? 1

Chapter 2   ReThink You 17

Chapter 3   ReThink Happiness 43

Chapter 4   ReThink Priorities 67

Chapter 5   ReThink Choices 89

Chapter 6   ReThink Relationships 121

Chapter 7   ReThink Generosity 143

Chapter 8   ReThink Impact 167

Using *ReThink* Life in Classes and Groups 185

ACKNOWLEDGMENTS

We want to thank our parents, Dr. Freddie and Barbara Gage, and Dr. Rod and Linda Masteller, who taught us how to rethink life.

We also want to thank our children—Rebecca, Ashlyn, and Luke—the ones we rethink life with every day.

We are deeply grateful for the staff and people of Fellowship Church Orlando. Your lives and stories inspire us. You have greatly touched our lives, and we are honored to partner with you in sharing the *reThink life* message with our city and the world.

PREFACE

Thoughts lead on to purpose, purpose leads on
to actions, actions form habits, habits decide
character, and character fixes our destiny.
—Tryon Edwards

Two people can face similar difficulties in their families
or careers, but they may respond in very different ways: one
is crushed under the weight of fear and hurt, while the other
thrives because he interprets the problem as an opportunity
to grow. What causes such widely varied responses to life?

It's all about our perception—how we think about the
important things in life. From the moment we're born, we
receive countless messages about the meaning of life. We
long for safety and purpose; these desires come as standard
equipment for human beings. We hear very loud voices that
tell us how to fulfill those desires. Too often, we don't even
stop to ask ourselves if the messages are good, right, and
true. We just buy into them without even thinking.

There have been a number of times in my (Rodney's)
life where I thought my way of thinking was right from my
perspective, only to discover later that I was very wrong.
One of my most embarrassing times was when my son,
Luke, asked me to drive him to one of Florida's original
theme parks, Jungle Adventures, for a school class field trip.
I was excited. I love alligators, wild animals, and swamp

rides! I was sure the day would create a lot of fun memories for Luke and me.

Early on the morning of the field trip, we met at the school. At the time, my son Luke was in a wheel chair (we'll talk about that later). Therefore we road separately in our car and we were instructed to follow the yellow school buses to our destination. There was no way to lose a big, yellow bus, so I didn't bother to get directions. Luke's teacher gave me her cell phone number, just in case we got separated. As we approached a major intersection, I decided to go around the bus in front of us so Luke could wave at his friends on the bus. When I pulled back into the lane, we were in front of the bus we'd been following. I noticed there were several other yellow school buses lined up at the stoplight. When the light turned green, the buses in front of us turned right and drove up the on-ramp of the interstate. I followed them, even though it seemed a bit odd that the buses behind us went straight instead of turning right. I really didn't give it too much thought, because I was confident I was doing the right thing by following the yellow school buses in front of me.

But soon doubts began to surface. What if we were supposed to go with the other buses? This was the way to Jungle Adventures, wasn't it? The route we were on sure seemed like the long way to get to our destination. Still, I kept reassuring myself that I was headed in the right direction because we were following the yellow school buses.

After a while, Luke grew a little impatient and asked the age-old question: "How much farther, Dad?"

Unwavering in my resolve to keep following the yellow buses, I responded, "Not long. Probably another ten minutes."

Twenty minutes later, the yellow school buses finally pulled into the parking lot. There was a huge gator head with a sign that read "Gatorland." With a perplexed look on his face, Luke exclaimed, "Wait a minute, Dad! This is not where our class is going! We're supposed to be going to Jungle Adventures."

About that time, my cell phone rang. Luke's teacher was wondering where we were. She said, "Mr. Gage, we've been here for nearly fifteen minutes, and we were getting concerned about you and Luke. Did you get lost?"

In a state of denial, I explained, "We're at Gatorland. Isn't this where we're supposed to be?"

"No," she said. "You're about thirty minutes across town from where we are. The field trip is at Jungle Adventures."

I asked her to give me the address, and then I looked up the directions on my phone. Luke and I raced across town to join his class. I'd done exactly what I thought was right, but it was very wrong. I had followed the buses, but I had followed the *wrong* buses.

Since this incident, I've thought about how many people live this way. We think we're following the right directions and making choices that will give us the security and fulfillment we long to experience, but we find ourselves chasing the wrong buses. Our perspective of life—our plans, goals, priorities, relationships, and direction—is shaped by many external factors, including our parents, the way we were raised, our peers, our life experiences (both good and bad), and a host of other influences. Too often, however, we miss the "big picture" of God's plans for our lives. King Solomon was one of the wisest men who ever lived. He warned, "There is a path before each person that seems right, but it ends in death" (Proverbs 14:12). We can try to convince others and ourselves that we're right, but that doesn't make it right. Seeing things from our limited, myopic perspective prevents us from reaching our full potential and fulfilling God's purposes for our lives.

We're writing this book to help people think more clearly, grasp the wonder and beauty of God's purpose, and take courageous steps to walk the road he wants us to walk. This message has inspired us with more hope and joy than we've ever experienced, and it has challenged our thinking in ways we never imagined. Learning to think the way God wants us to think isn't easy, but it's the path to real life, joy, peace, and love.

In this book, both of us—Rodney and Michelle—are partners. God has captured our hearts with his truth and love, and we want to share it with you. When we tell stories, we'll make sure you know which of us is telling them. But we want you to know that the message of this book comes from both our hearts.

Each chapter unpacks principles that help us think more clearly and take bold steps to live by God's truth. At the end of each chapter, you'll find three elements of application: perspective, choices, and impact. As our thoughts are shaped around God's truth, we'll see that we have clear choices to make about the things that matter in life. As we make countless choices to live for God instead of the empty promises of the world, we'll stand up and stand out. People will notice, and God will use us to make a difference in their lives. There's no greater privilege.

Along the way, you'll have lots of questions. That's entirely normal. Whenever we learn a new sport, a new software program, or a new recipe, there's always a learning curve. Don't be discouraged if you don't get it right the first time. We certainly didn't! God is delighted that you're on the journey to know him, love him, and serve him by learning to think his thoughts. We're pretty thrilled too.

———

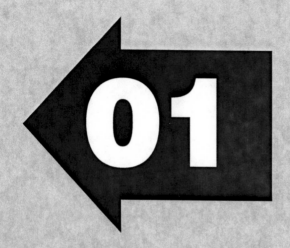

CHAPTER 1

Why ReThink Life?

We do not see things as they are.
We see them as we are.
—The Talmud

On Memorial Day weekend a few years ago, Michelle and I drove to Miami on the Florida Turnpike for a getaway cruise to celebrate our twentieth wedding anniversary and the tenth anniversary of Fellowship Church Orlando. I noticed a traffic sign next to the highway that indicted there was going to be congestion ahead. I thought it said to expect a two-hour delay, but since it didn't say if the delay was due to construction or an accident, I thought it was an error. I said to Michelle, "Surely they wouldn't have workers working on a construction site with all the holiday traffic on a Memorial Day weekend. And if there's been a wreck, it wouldn't take them two hours to clean up the mess."

About forty miles down the road, we came to a complete stop. It was like we had pulled into a parking lot. Out to the horizon, we looked at a sea of red lights ahead of us. For what seemed like an eternity, we didn't move an inch. After about fifteen minutes, people began to get out of their cars. They sat on the side railing of the highway, smoking cigarettes, pulling out their coolers, having a drink, talking on their cell phones, and walking their dogs. The delay may not have been a big inconvenience for them, but we had to get to the ship! Soon our blood began to boil. We were frustrated, angry, and upset. We couldn't sit back and enjoy hanging out with these people because we simply had to be somewhere at a certain time or our plans would radically change.

Michelle got on her phone's GPS to find the nearest exit. It was nowhere close. Our only option was to turn around and go all the way back to the point where we got on the highway so we could take a different road. But we were stuck in the far left lane. About two hundred yards in front of us, a few cars and SUVs were cutting through the median in a lane reserved for "Official Use Only." It looked like a good plan, but we couldn't get there; we were trapped. I began to slowly maneuver our car and honk our horn, motioning for the people in front of us and behind us to move to give us some room. Finally, we began to work our way onto the shoulder and slowly move forward. People had to shut their car doors and move their cars out of our way so we could get through. You can imagine the faces, hand gestures, and comments!

We finally made it to the U-turn in the median and got on the highway going the opposite direction. As we drove for miles back the way we'd come, we saw thousands of cars that formed a huge parking lot on the Florida Turnpike. It reminded us of a scene often played out in people's lives: thousands of people getting stuck on the highway of life.

We could have stayed stuck on the highway, but we were determined to find a different way. We weren't content to just let things happen naturally. We wanted to be objective about our situation, recognize the fact that we had to take bold action, and then find a way to get out of that mess.

This experience is an example of what it means to rethink Life.

TWO ROADS

One day, Jesus taught a crowd of people on a hillside. In the course of his talk on "life," he used a word picture to describe the two roads. He referred to one as the "broad" road. It was the easy path, and many people were on it. (Matthew 7:13–14).

The broad road Jesus described represents the world's value of the relentless pursuit of success, pleasure, and approval. The reason so many people are on this road is that it's easy to find. Everyone seems to be headed in this direction, and it's the path of least resistance. It's the "normal" road that promises everything that we could possibly want in life: career success, friendships, good education, entertainment, religion, freedom, pleasure, and fun. What else could anyone possibly want? This road has to be broad to accommodate all the travelers.

I can imagine the crowd of people listening to Jesus that day, nodding their heads in agreement, perhaps leaning over to their neighbor with a smile and saying something like, "I'm glad I'm on that road, aren't you?"

Suddenly, Jesus made a statement that rattled their cages: "The masses of people traveling on the broad road are ultimately headed for destruction. It's a road that leads to disappointment." Then Jesus told them about another road—a very different one. Jesus described this road as "narrow." Only a few people find it, but for those who do, it offers the ultimate destination: a present hope and an eternal reward unlike anything this world can offer. The journey on the narrow road isn't free of problems, but it's a road marked with hope, forgiveness, inner peace, joy, and true happiness unlike anything people have ever experienced. When the crowd heard Jesus describe the two roads, they began to rethink their situations; they noticed which road they were on and the direction they were traveling. And then they had a choice.

Maybe you're thinking the same thing. You may see yourself on the broad road. You may have fallen into the trap of just blending in, staying stuck in a rut, and trying to keep up the hectic pace of the crowd that's traveling down the broad road. Unfortunately, even though it appears to be popular and appealing, the broad road isn't the one God intended for us to take.

We are eternal beings. We were made by God and for God. Any time we focus on the temporal things in life, we come up short, because the temporal things ultimately can't satisfy. There is nothing wrong with success. We have many friends who are high-capacity leaders, highly respected by the average crowd because of their achievements and financial successes. But the wisest among them don't expect success and wealth to make them happy or fill the hole in their hearts. They are completely committed to Christ and have made him the primary focus of their lives. Even though they are very successful in the way the world measures success, they know that their success is a gift from God.

Their greatest joy is using their success as an opportunity to invest their time, talents, and financial resources in eternal things. They're different. They've chosen to live by following the narrow road. While there's nothing wrong with possessions and relationships, many people attempt to find security by filling their lives with material things, relationships, or their work to meet needs that only God can fulfill. The broad road promises the moon, but it eventually produces only dust.

How can we tell which road we're on? What are some indications that we're on the wrong road? We get a glimpse into our hearts when we experience difficulties. If we have a disproportionate reaction to failure, rejection, and disappointment, it may reveal that we're placing too much security or dependence in the wrong things.

DIFFICULTIES: A WINDOW INTO OUR SOULS

Life's heartaches have a way of surfacing our hidden values, perceptions, and beliefs. We see this happen almost daily in the news. When tragedy strikes, lives are changed in an instant.

Almost weekly, we meet people who tell us about the loss of a job or a home, a health crisis, spousal abandonment, or the death of a loved one. Suddenly their lives are turned upside down. When unexpected crises occur, they force us to stop and rethink the very meaning of life.

I (Michelle) can identify with people who experience calamities. Our family too has been forced to stop and rethink a lot in the past few years. Several years ago, we faced a medical crisis with Luke, the youngest of our three children, and our world was rocked. Like most families with children, we had a very busy schedule. Keeping up with our son's schedule alone kept us hopping. We took Luke to ball practice several nights a week and watched him play games on Saturday mornings. In the spring of that year, Luke began to complain of pain in his leg and knee. Because a ball had hit him in one of his practices, we thought he must have bruised or possibly broken something, but X-rays revealed that nothing was broken. Still, he continued to experience pain and began to limp. Doctors wrote it off as "growing pains," but we weren't convinced. After a few months had passed, his limp became more severe, and the pain didn't go away.

A friend who is an orthopedist told Rodney to bring Luke to his house one evening so he could take a look at Luke's leg. After examining Luke, the doctor told Rodney he had a hunch about the diagnosis, but he would need an MRI to confirm it. When he saw the MRI of Luke's hip, the orthopedist confirmed that he had a rare hip disease called

Perthes, in which the ball of the femur slowly dies. If left untreated, the ball can completely crush under the person's normal weight, causing major problems for a lifetime.

After much research, we found a world-renowned specialist in Perthes who practiced medicine about an hour-and-a-half away from our home. We immediately made an appointment, but we weren't prepared for the news we heard. The doctor felt that the best form of treatment for Luke wasn't traditional surgery or leg braces but for Luke to be placed in a wheelchair for two to four years. There would be no running, jumping, or playing any sports. Needless to say, our world was turned upside-down.

I can remember walking out of the hospital that day, pushing Luke in a wheelchair and trying to hold back the tears as I saw other crippled children in their wheelchairs. We would never see the world the same again. It was heartbreaking to realize that he would be immobilized during the most active years of his life. Gradually, we began to realize that God had a greater plan for our son and for our family. Even though we didn't understand it at the time, we knew God was ultimately in control. For over two years, Luke was in a wheelchair. Over the course of those years, many people told us that Luke's life was an inspiration to them as they went through their own personal challenges.

Thanks to answered prayer and God's healing, Luke is out of his wheelchair, enjoying the freedom of walking and running again. But his healing is only part of the story. Luke has a richer, deeper perspective about life that most young boys will never have. He sees difficult situations and physically challenged individuals with a different set of eyes. Our whole family has learned from this experience. Because of it, we all have a different perspective on life. As a family, it forced us to stop and rethink what's important. We learned that God wants to take our circumstances and challenges and use them, not only to fulfill his greater purposes but also to use them for our benefit and the benefit of others.

It's easy to feel like the unplanned and unwanted circumstances we face in life's journey are unfair, but we need to remember that God thinks differently from us, and he sees our lives from an eternal point of view. The normal people traveling on the broad road can only see what's tangible and visible. They only see what's directly in front of them from their own limited perspectives. That's why unplanned, unwanted circumstances can seem so devastating. When we place our security or happiness in the wrong things, it's easy to feel frustrated, disappointed, or even completely disillusioned with life.

Maybe that is where you are right now. Perhaps, you've spent your life trying to be normal and fill your life with success, pleasure, and approval. You've been traveling down the broad road chasing the American Dream, like most people. You may have thought that happiness could be found in your position, pleasure, or possessions. Maybe you've put your trust in a person or group of people to find your worth and significance. If so, it's time to rethink the direction of your life and seriously consider making a U-turn. Life is too short and the consequences are too big to get it wrong. It's time to get off the broad road that everyone sees as normal and get on the narrow road that gives you God's eternal perspective for your life.

MAKING A CHANGE

How do we make this switch? How do we choose a different road for our lives? The Bible teaches us . . .

Don't copy the behavior and customs of this world, but let God transform you into a new person by changing the way you think. Then, you will learn to know God's will for you, which is good and pleasing and perfect. (Romans 12: 2)

According to this verse the change begins with the battlefield going on in our minds. The "behavior and customs of this world" press us into their mold, lie to us about what's really important, and keep us locked in mediocrity. Changing the way we think changes everything!

Some people reading this book already have a relationship with God, but they've been drifting down the wrong road. They've been listening to the powerful but misleading messages from negative friends or persuasive advertising in our culture, and they've believed too many deceptions about their promises. If you're one of these people, make a new commitment to get back on the right road. This book will help you clarify your thinking and make better choices. It'll be the adventure of your life. Don't miss it! Make a choice to refocus and retrain your mind to rethink life.

But some people reading this book haven't made this primary link with the God of the universe. The incredible news is that you can! God loves you and wants you to enjoy life to the fullest. The only way that can happen is to listen to his voice and follow his path. You can't do it on your own, and you don't have to. When you become a genuine follower of Jesus Christ, the Spirit of God will live in you and guide you as you listen to him. If you're willing to exit the broad road and take the narrow road Jesus described, then tell God what you want. He delights in answering this kind of prayer!

God promises that he will draw close to us if we will draw close to him. He promises not only to forgive us, but also to renew our hearts and give us a fresh start. When we begin to see our lives from an eternal perspective, every moment, every task, and every relationship takes on new meaning. Our sense of identity, attitude, priorities, choices, relationships, money, and purpose take on new meaning.

Unfortunately, many people who claim to be Christians have given in to the temptation to blend in with the crowd. They settle for second best rather than experience God's best. That's tragic and unnecessary. God has so much more for us! We struggle with this temptation every day, like everyone else. Too many Christians view God as a compartment of their lives. They only surrender a part of their lives to God, giving him an hour or two of their week while living the rest of their weekly routine in the pursuit of self-absorbed dreams.

But God's not just a *part* of our lives. He *is* life, and he wants to be at the center of our lives. When we truly know him, our motivations are transformed. When we experience his love and forgiveness, our hearts are

> Living to know and serve him should be our greatest pursuit and number-one priority, not an afterthought or a weekly obligation.

filled with gratitude. We want to please him in everything we do. The Christian life is about knowing God and making him known. Life is all about him. Living to know and serve him should be our greatest pursuit and number-one priority, not an afterthought or a weekly obligation.

STANDING UP AND STANDING OUT

God has created us to experience so much more than what our culture considers normal. Rather than blending in and conforming to the thinking and behaviors of the world,

God has created us to stand out. Even though we are to live *in* the world, we aren't to be *of* the world. He has called us to live differently from the norm.

When we moved to Orlando from Dallas, we were in need of a family-size vehicle that would be good for transporting kids here, there, and everywhere—along with all their stuff. I (Rodney) have a friend who sells cars. He assured me he could find us a vehicle at the auction. I gave him a list of possible vehicles and a budget. He said that as long as we were patient and flexible with colors and features he could get us a good deal. We gave him the green light to find us a car.

A few weeks later, he called us and announced, "I found your car."

"What is it?" I asked.

"It's a 2000 GMC Yukon XL," he explained. "It's in mint condition, practically brand new, with less than twenty thousand miles."

"Awesome! What color is it?" I asked.

"It's bright red," he said.

Surprised, I asked, "Bright red?" (Bright red is a color I associated with sports cars, like a Ferrari.) "I don't know about that," I reasoned aloud. "I like red, but I don't know if I like *that much* red."

"Trust me. You'll love it!" he assured me.

I told him to go for it, so he bought a bright-red Yukon XL that had been used to pull a horse trailer. The former owner had installed special yellow lights—similar to those on a huge semitruck—on top of the vehicle. (My friend, the car salesman, had failed to tell me about those.) Needless to say, everyone could see this bright-red truck with huge lights a mile away.

Fast-forward to ten years later. Michelle and her bright-red Yukon became known among all the carpool kids as "Mama G and Big Bertha." And I often referred to the vehicle as the "fire truck." Everywhere Michelle went, she stood out from among all the other vehicles with her bright-red suburban with its obnoxious headlights.

We eventually got rid of the vehicle. We replaced "Big Bertha" with another pre-owned Suburban. Only this time, we got Michelle a black one. After she had driven her new vehicle for a few weeks, she commented that she missed her bright-red truck with its obnoxious lights. When I asked why, she said, "Because I don't stand out any more."

The connection may not seem obvious, but this is the way God has called us to live. While the norm is to conform, we are to stand out and be different—to be transformers. When we begin living for the eternal instead of the temporal, and we make a

> While the norm is to conform, we are to stand out and be different

commitment to be a light in the world, we'll experience true joy and fulfillment, and we'll have a profound impact on others. To take a dramatic step onto the narrow road, we don't have to have all the answers. We can't know what's a mile ahead or even around the next bend. We just need to know that we're on the right road and Jesus is with us. Martin Luther King Jr. observed, "Faith is taking the first step, even when you don't see the whole staircase."[1]

Are you ready to get off the broad road? It's not going to be easy, but trust me; the narrow road is worth the effort. Taking a different path will be an incredible journey, but like every adventure, it's a risk worth taking. Fasten your seat belt, because you're about to take the ride of your life!

What does it mean to rethink life? We need to realize that our lives consist of two dates. On our tombstones, people will see the date we were born and a date we died. In between those two dates will be a dash. To rethink life is to ask the question: How are we going to use the dash? When we learn to see every moment of our lives from God's eternal perspective, we can fulfill the very purpose for which we were created.

Life isn't just a dress rehearsal; it's the real thing. We get one shot to get it right. Learning to live life from God's perspective influences the choices we make here on earth. Our choices determine the impact we will make in the lives of others and for his glory.

> Life isn't just a dress rehearsal; it's the real thing. We get one shot to get it right. Learning to live life from God's perspective influences the choices we make here on earth.

Think about it . . .

Perspective

1. Identify a situation in which you were convinced you were right about something, only to discover later that you were wrong. (If you are working through these questions with others, have fun with this one.)
2. Think about your favorite commercials. What are their surface promises? What are the subtle but powerful implied promises of true fulfillment and real love?
3. How would you describe the broad way and the narrow way? What do they look like in people's daily lives?
4. Is Jesus really worth putting in the center of our lives? Why or why not?

5. What are some reasons people tend to compartmentalize God instead of loving him with their whole hearts, all day, every day?

Choice

6. Read Romans 12:1-2. What are some things you can do to transform your thinking?
7. What are some practical ways to know that your mind is being transformed? (Think about your responses to opportunities and problems, your love for people who naturally annoy you, your desire for your life to count, etc.)

Impact

8. What does it mean for us to live differently from the norm or to be a "light"? Is that attractive to you? Why or why not?
9. Who is one person in your world who needs you to step in to show God's love and strength? What will you do to help? When will you do it?

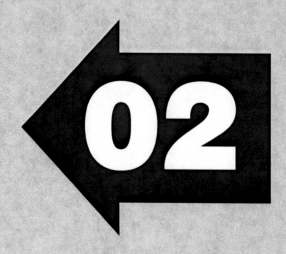

CHAPTER 2

ReThink You

No one can make us feel inferior without our
permission.
—Eleanor Roosevelt

The way we view ourselves determines our responses
to every person, opportunity, and challenge. If we find a
radical security in the unconditional love of God, we
develop a wonderful blend of contentment and passion. We
don't spend our time defending ourselves or competing with
others. We are deeply convinced that we are loved, forgiven,
and accepted, so we can relax, care for those around us, and
pursue God for all we're worth!

Taking pictures has never been easier. Today, cell phones
and computers have built-in cameras, so we can take fun
and quick pics any time. Our family loves to play around
with the pictures we take. We've gotten a big kick out of the
Photo Booth application that came on our iMac computer.
Apple has provided a lot of entertainment for us. We've
snapped pictures of ourselves and then doctored them with
Photo Booth effects that make us look . . . well, really funny.
Among our family favorites are the Bent Pole, Obamafy, and
Freak Show effects in this program. The results are hilarious.
Our kids delight in stretching, magnifying, and swirling our
images. This app has given us many opportunities to laugh
at ourselves.

But apps like Photo Booth create inaccurate, contorted
images—they're not true reflections of who we are. While
we laugh at these distortions, many of us have suffered from
another kind of image distortion. Tragically, many of us
live our entire lives with a grossly distorted and inaccurate
picture of who we really are. We don't appreciate our true
worth and beauty. Like an image distorted by Photo Booth,
we see ourselves as strange, out-of-place, and unacceptable.

We'd laugh at the image we see of ourselves, but it hurts too much. We never reach our God-given potential because we continually live in bondage to the lies we believe about ourselves. Instead, we live with pride and arrogance because we're trying to cover up our flaws, or we live under a dark cloud of shame and self-condemnation because we realize we've failed so miserably. And some of us are creative enough to vacillate between arrogance and shame!

To rethink our identity, we need to see ourselves from God's perspective—as valuable, forgivable, and capable.

RETHINK YOU . . . AS VALUABLE

Imagine me handing you a crisp, new, one-hundred-dollar bill. Would you want it? Suppose I crumpled it up so it didn't look as nice as when it first came from the mint. Would you still want it? Sure you would! But wait. What if I took it outside and threw it on the ground and stomped on it so that it got so stained that the picture on the bill was barely recognizable.

> Your value has been established by the Creator of the universe, and no one can take that away from you.

Would you still want it? Of course! God sees you as valuable, no matter what challenges and difficulties have entered your life and tarnished your original, mint condition. Even though you feel crumpled, stomped, and stained, you're still a hundred-dollar bill. Just as that hundred-dollar bill maintains its value, you never lose your value. Your value has been established by the Creator of the universe, and no one can take that away from you.

Our identity is incredibly important, but most of us would rather have a root canal than take a look inside the Pandora's box of our hearts to see what's really there. Objectivity, however, isn't optional. The process of rethinking our lives begins with a courageous look at the very core of who we are and how we perceive ourselves. If we're honest about what we find, it will get messy—even ugly—but the process will unveil the lies that hold us captive. But it's not all bad news. It will also reveal liberating truth that we are deeply loved, totally accepted, and completely forgiven by God. Then we have a choice: to reject the lies and live in the truth.

To see yourself as valuable and, in fact, priceless in the eyes of God, ask yourself these questions about your self-perception:

- How do you see yourself: as a valuable treasure or damaged goods, a masterpiece of God's creation or a disgraceful person?
- Do you see yourself as a paper cup—disposable, easily used, and then thrown away? Or do your see yourself as a crystal goblet that has high value and is treated with respect?
- How do you feel about yourself? What words do you use to describe yourself—especially when you've failed and no one is around to hear you?
- As you reflected on these questions, how did you come up with your answers? Whose voice did you hear in your head?

Many of us obsess over our inadequacies and flaws. Messages from the world of advertising, competition, and gossip tell us we don't measure up and need to change to be acceptable. In fact, in any given year, Americans spend over a hundred and sixty billion dollars on beauty. We spend more on beauty than we do on educating our children. We spend this enormous amount of money on makeup, skin and hair care, fragrances, cosmetic surgery, health clubs, and diet aids. We live in a culture consumed with trying to create the perfect façade. We believe that if we can look a certain way, drive a certain car, live in a certain neighborhood, earn a certain title in our careers, and impress a certain group of people, we can find happiness and fulfillment. We think that "image is reality," so we devote our time, money, and energy in crafting our image for the world to see. And before we shake our heads at "those people out there," we need to look at ourselves very carefully. Most Christians are caught up in this deception just as much as anyone else. God wants so much more for us than this!

I (Michelle) have a friend who works for a medical spa in Dallas where people can get services or treatments to improve their appearance. She finds it amazing in today's economy—when people are struggling financially—that so many still come to the spa and spend their entire paychecks to get treatments designed to make them look younger and more like the images they see on the covers of fashion magazines. These people—mostly women—know they can't afford these services, but they're convinced they can't live without them. There's nothing wrong with having nice clothes, wearing makeup, and looking our best—as long as those things don't take first place in our hearts. As long as they're secondary, we can enjoy them with a good heart and a clear conscience. The real source of our confidence isn't in these things; it's in the radical, wonderful love of God.

> When we see ourselves as God sees us, we experience true Godfidence.

When we see ourselves as God sees us, we experience true Godfidence.

Too often, we obsess over the things we believe will make us beautiful, because we're sure they will give us true happiness. The problem is that this strategy never works. No matter how much money we spend on beauty treatments or how we work at having a more beautiful body, we'll always feel inferior to the gorgeous models in the ads (and maybe even the beautiful people sitting near us at church). No matter how much time and money we spend on looking great, we will always need the next cosmetic treatment, because the last one didn't correct every flaw. We'll need more diets pills, because the last batch didn't take off enough pounds, and another trip to the salon for the latest hair style, because the last one didn't turn out quite right. We become consumed with creating a false image of ourselves, and in the process, we lose sight of who we really are. These misguided efforts destroy our identity and mar our true beauty.

Why do we obsess over our appearance and focus so much of our time and energy on external things? More importantly, why do we who claim to know the God of the universe—who loves us dearly—look to the culture's solutions to find happiness? Take time to rethink the steps you take to achieve beauty, success, and happiness. Answer these questions:

- Is your self-image based on what the world says or what God says? How can you tell?
- Does the world or the Word of God shape your perspective of who you are and how you see yourself? What are the messages of each one?
- Are you better off when you listen to commercials or God's voice? What's the difference?

Israel's first king, Saul, was the tallest and most handsome man in the land. Everyone was awed by his appearance, but he proved to be a poor king. Finally, God sent the prophet Samuel to Jesse's house to anoint the next king of Israel, but God didn't tell the prophet which of Jesse's sons was the new leader. Jesse paraded his sons in front of the old prophet, and one of them was particularly impressive. Samuel was sure this was the one. But the Lord told him, "Don't judge by his appearance or height, for I have rejected him. The Lord doesn't see things the way you see them. People judge by outward appearance, but the Lord looks at the heart" (1 Samuel 16:7).

> People judge by outward appearance, but the Lord looks at the heart

We go to the mountains and the coast to enjoy nature, but God calls *us* the pinnacle of creation! Jesus didn't die for trees and manatees he gave his life for us. When the people following Christ needed reassurance of God's vast and endless love, he told them, "Look at the birds. They don't need to plant or harvest or put food in barns because God feeds them. And you are far more valuable to him than any birds!" (Luke 12:24).

As believers, we're too blessed to be obsessed. The love and acceptance of God overwhelms feelings of doubt and inadequacy. Why don't we bask in our identity as beloved children of God? Because our minds are so cluttered with the messages of the world. We value the opinions of others instead of the opinion of God. For too long we've sacrificed inner peace, joy, and happiness by allowing the world to shape our self-image. Without realizing it, we've chosen to be conformers instead of embracing the life of a transformed child of God. We'll never discover our true identity and find real happiness in our culture's value system. It's like following the wrong bus to Gatorland instead of our real destination. The voices of our culture sound reasonable, and in fact, everyone else is listening to them. They sound seductive and alluring, but they lead to heartache. These voices constantly beat us down and tell us to compare ourselves to others—a game we can never win, because there's always somebody prettier, more handsome, stronger, richer, and more gifted than we are. Incessantly the voices whisper that we're inferior and can't measure up. In those fleeting moments when we compare favorably, we become prideful and feel superior to those around us. This perception alienates us from people and from God. So, even when we win, we lose.

If we value the glitz and glamour that the product-pushers say we must have, we'll be disappointed, because what the world offers is short-lived and can't ultimately satisfy the deepest longings of our souls. But when we allow God to control our thinking, we become transformed. We begin to live differently. We learn to like—and even love—ourselves, because we begin to see ourselves as beautiful creations made in the image of the Father who greatly loves and values us.

The Scriptures paint a glowing picture of God's view of us. In the Old Testament, Isaiah quoted God: "Because I am God, your personal God, I paid a huge price for you. That's how much you mean to mean to me. That's how much I love you. I'd sell off the whole world to get you back, trade creation just for you" (Isaiah 43:3-4 MSG).

When the people wondered if God had forgotten about them, Isaiah told them what God had tenderly said to assure them: "Never! Can a mother forget her nursing child? Can she feel no love for the child she has borne? But even if that were possible, I would not forget you! See, I have written your name on the palms of my hands" (Isaiah 49:15-16).

And in the New Testament, Paul wrote, "God purchased you at a high price. Don't be enslaved by the things of the world" (1 Corinthians 7:23).

Peter described our identity this way: "You are a chosen people. You are royal priests, a holy nation, God's very own possession. As a result, you can show others the goodness of God, for he called you out of the darkness into his wonderful light" (1 Peter 2:9).

These passages of Scripture are just a taste of the wonderful, encouraging, life-giving truths in God's Word about our identity as his dearly beloved children. Don't miss it! You are so valuable to God that he purchased you—all of who you are, inside and out, including your poor self-image and all of your flaws—with the blood of his very own Son, Jesus Christ. What does this high price and extreme payment tell you? Simply that you have infinite worth to the God of the universe. When you feel inferior, "less than," or like a misfit, stop and think about these passages. Don't condemn or devalue yourself because you feel you're unworthy to be loved, forgiven, accepted, or valued. God wants you to understand that you are more valuable to him than the stars in the sky. You are worth more to him than all the gold, diamonds, real estate, and fine things the world has ever treasured. He paid the highest price imaginable. Why? To demonstrate the depth of his love for you. He bought your freedom so you can live a transformed life. When Jesus wanted to explain the nature of God, he said, "For God so loved the world that He gave His one and only Son, that whoever believes in Him shall not perish but have eternal life" (John 3:16 NIV).

What do we know about God's amazing love? We know:

- It's consistent.

  God's love never wavers. He loves you now and always. There is no "he loves me, he loves me not" when you are in a relationship with God. The Christians in Rome needed reassurance about the extent of God's love for them, so Paul wrote, "For I am convinced that neither death, nor life, nor angels, nor principalities, nor things present, nor things to come, nor powers, nor height, nor depth, nor any other created thing, will be able to separate us from the love of God, which is in Christ Jesus our Lord" (Romans 8:38-39 NASB).

- It's unconditional.

  God's love and acceptance doesn't depend on you. God doesn't say, "I love you *if*..." You don't win the love of God by being good enough or trying to measure up to any worldly or religious standards. The Bible says we all have sinned and have no way of measuring up apart from the saving work of

> God's love and acceptance doesn't depend on you. God doesn't say, "I love you if..."

Jesus Christ. Paul explained, "For the wages of sin is death, but the free gift of God is eternal life through Christ Jesus our Lord" Romans 6:23 NIV). The paradox of the gospel is that the sinless Son of God paid for our sins so we could be forgiven, cleansed, and adopted into God's family. Jesus took the punishment we deserved so that we could receive the love and acceptance we don't deserve. That's what grace is all about! God doesn't wink at our sin like a benevolent but senile grandfather. He looked at our sin square in the face, pronounced judgment on it, and then paid the supreme penalty in full. At the cross, God's justice and mercy meet.

God loves everyone, and Christ's death is available to all people on the planet, but the people who come to Jesus and enjoy his love are the ones who are humble enough to admit their need for him. The proud religious leaders during Jesus' time on earth hated him and despised his compassion for people, but the misfits and outcasts flocked to him. They sensed that his love, kindness, and grace were far greater than their own sins and flaws. They gladly received his love, and they loved him in return.

As you've read these passages, stories, and explanations, what has gone on in your mind and heart? Did you feel thrilled to be reminded (or to know for the first time) that you greatly matter to God? Or did you feel resistant, or even angry, because you have never sensed the joy and freedom of being loved by God—or by anyone else? No matter who you are or where you've come from, don't give up on God's extravagant love for you. Start where you are. Be ruthlessly honest with him about your doubts and fears, and ask him to reveal his kindness to you. Our prayer for you is the same one that Paul prayed for the Christians in Ephesus: "May you have the power to understand, as all God's people should, how wide, how long, how high, and how deep his love is. May you experience the love of Christ, though it is too great to understand fully. Then you will be made complete with all the fullness of life and power that comes from God" (Ephesians 3:18-19).

RETHINK YOU . . . AS FORGIVABLE

All of Scripture describes the wonderful fact of God's forgiveness. The sacrifices in the Old Testament pointed to a day when the Lamb of God would be the final sacrifice for the sins of the world, including our sins. Christ's payment for sin on the cross set us free—free to love him and free to be the people he wants us to be. God longs for us to live in complete freedom—knowing and understanding who we are in Christ—so we can brightly and radiantly reflect the character of Jesus Christ. When our identity is based on the level of success, pleasure, and approval of others, we can never be free. We always wonder if we've done enough. But if our self-image is deeply rooted in the amazing grace of God, our hearts experience the confidence of his love.

If God's forgiveness is so vast and deep, why do so many people continue to live in bondage? Why do so many people struggle day after day to find a semblance of peace and meaning when the cross of Jesus provides all the freedom and purpose we could ever want?

Rethink your perception of God's forgiveness:

- How do people think, feel, and act when they're sure their sins are forgiven?
- Are you amazed at the depth of God's forgiveness, or do you fall short of enjoying the fullness of God's grace?
- What keeps you from living a life of freedom—fear, guilt, shame, or doubt? How might these cloud your mind and shape your attitude?
- Are there any painful past experiences that keep you from believing that God forgives you and is crazy about you? If so, how do these past experiences affect you?

God not only sees us as valuable; he also sees us as forgivable. His forgiveness doesn't depend on our efforts to earn it. Jesus paid the price in full at the cross. The gospel, then, is both the best news and the worst news we'll ever hear. It means that our sins grieved God so badly that we were alienated from him—hopeless and alone. That's bad news! But God didn't leave us in our predicament. Jesus Christ stepped out of heaven to live and die for us. He values us too much to leave us as helpless outcasts. He has taken the only step that would work, the death of a sinless sacrifice, to pay the price we could never pay on our own.

What did Christ's sacrifice accomplish for us? Paul explained, "Even before he made the world, God loved us and chose us in Christ to be holy and without fault in his eyes. God decided in advance to adopt us into his own family by bringing us to himself through Jesus Christ. This is what he wanted to do, and it gave him great pleasure" (Ephesians 1:4-5).

Sadly, many people today hear the truth about the cross and God's offer of forgiveness, but they shake their heads and walk away. They think, "That may be true for other people but not for me. I wish I could believe that God could forgive my sins, but they're too big and too ugly." There are forces for good in the world, and there are forces of evil. The "enemy of our souls," Satan, uses an array of devices to keep people away from God's grace and a transformed life. He deceives, tempts, and accuses. He is "the father of lies," who uses the deception of our culture to convince us that God only accepts people who prove they've earned a spot in his family.

Is that how the Bible describes God's love, forgiveness, and acceptance? Certainly not! Satan also tempts us with money and power—assuring us that these things will fill the gaping holes in our hearts. And finally, our enemy accuses us with slurs that we'll never measure up to God's standard, so we might as well give up. Actually, he's right. We can't ever measure up, but we don't have to, because Someone did it for us. Jesus stood in our place, paid the price we couldn't pay, and set us free from the penalty of God's just judgment of our sins. One of the problems is that when Satan accuses us, he uses our own voice to condemn us. From our own minds we hear, "God could never love someone like you. You're a failure—a nobody. You might as well give up." And quite often, Satan uses condemning voices from our past.

Almost every week when I (Rodney) talk about the incredible love and forgiveness of God, someone comes up to tell me, "Rodney, you just don't understand my past. You don't understand what I've done. You have no idea what kinds of mistakes I've made." Many of these people are convinced that life is rotten because they deserve it to be rotten. They think they had it coming, so they beat themselves up and live under an oppressive, dark cloud of self-condemnation. Their past has determined their present. They fail to understand that all our sins—past, present, and future—are wiped away by the blood of Christ. The Bible says that God has not only forgiven them but has also gotten rid of them forever. Through Isaiah, God told his people, "I—yes, I alone—am the one who blots out your sins for my own sake and will never think of them again" (Isaiah 43:25).

We will only experience God's wonderful forgiveness if we admit we're deeply flawed and sinful. Then he delights to show us how much he loves us, the extent of his forgiveness, and our new status as his dear children. Honesty is the first step in our experience of God's great love.

RETHINK YOU . . . AS CAPABLE

When we watch horse races like the Kentucky Derby, we marvel at the grace, power, and speed of the horses—even those that finish in the back of the pack. They didn't arrive at Churchill Downs that day by accident. Their owners carefully bred them to be champions. Stud fees can be half a million dollars. When they were colts, some of these horses appeared to be nothing special, but their owners and trainers knew they had the bloodlines of winners. Slowly, the young horses' potentials began to emerge.

In the same way, each of us comes from the spiritual bloodlines of champions of the faith. Abraham answered God's call and was faithful even when everything looked hopeless. Joseph trusted God through the darkest days anyone can imagine, and God used him to rescue his family and a nation from starvation. Moses freed God's people from slavery in Egypt and led them to the Promised Land. Samson demonstrated his strength to win mighty battles. David led "the mighty men" in war and unified the land. Solomon built a glorious temple for God's presence. Esther risked her life to save God's people from slaughter. After Jesus was raised from the tomb, the eleven disciples gave their lives heroically to take the message of grace to the whole world.

Countless men and women through the ages have taken bold steps and risked everything for Christ's cause. But that's not all. Our bloodlines go back even further and run even deeper. God has adopted us as his own children, so he is our Father. And Jesus is our elder brother who gave his life for us. Peter describes us this way: "You are a chosen people. You are royal priests, a holy nation, God's very own possession. As a result, you can show others the goodness of God, for he called you out of the darkness into his wonderful light" (1 Peter 2:9). None of us is ordinary; we all carry the DNA of royalty, warriors, and champions.

Psychologists tell us that a child needs two things to develop a healthy, strong self-image: love and a sense of being capable. It's no different for adults. All of us need to know that what we do matters and that we do it well. In Paul's glowing explanation of the power of the gospel in his letter to the Ephesians, he doesn't stop with the fact that God has set us free. He explains that God has carefully crafted us so that our lives really count. Paul wrote, "For we are God's masterpiece. He has created us anew in Christ Jesus, so we can do the good things he planned for us long ago" (Ephesians 2:10).

"For we are God's Masterpiece"

How do you feel when you stand in front of a Rembrandt painting or one of Michelangelo's incredible sculptures? When we look at a great work of art, we're amazed at the skill of the artist and the beauty of his creation. We call these works of art *masterpieces*. That's the word Paul uses to describe each of us! We are His *magnum opus*—the best and greatest, his most renowned achievement!

Do you believe you're God's masterpiece? You are. Do you realize he has shaped your experiences, intelligence, and skills so you can make a difference in people's lives? He has. One of our jobs as Christians is to uncover the skills and discover the roles God has for us. In many ways, it's like finding the right job after we graduate from high school or college. We may not get it right the first time, but even our failed attempts help us clarify our sense of calling in God's kingdom. His purpose isn't limited to the walls of a church for a few hours a week. Most of us serve God in very diverse places—in our offices, fields, homes, schools, and neighborhoods. We may have structured ministries with titles, or our primary role in God's kingdom may be more fluid and spontaneous. But make no mistake: all of us have an important role to play, and God is equipping us to play it well. He gives us the ability to lead, to comfort, to teach, to help, and to equip others to accomplish what God has given them to do. Playing our part in God's great work of changing lives is one of the highest privileges we can imagine.

> Make no mistake: all of us have an important role to play, and God is equipping us to play it well.

A professional golfer was invited by the King of Saudi Arabia to play in a celebrity golf tournament. The king's private jet picked up the golfer and flew him from the United States to Saudi Arabia. After several days of participating in the golf tournament and being overwhelmed by the lavish hospitality, the golfer prepared to go home to the States. The king approached the golfer and said, "I want you to know that we were honored to have you participate in our golf tournament. I would like to give you a token of our appreciation, a gift that will serve as a reminder so that you may always remember your experience here in Saudi Arabia."

The golfer tried to downplay his participation in the tournament. He said, "It was a privilege for me to come here. Please don't feel obligated to give me anything."

But the king insisted. "No, I want to give you something. Tell me, what would be a meaningful gift for you?"

The golfer replied, "Well, I collect golf clubs. If you want to get me a golf club, that would be nice."

As he boarded the private jet and flew back home, the golfer thought about his conversation with the king. The golfer fantasized that the king might give him a solid gold putter, perhaps with his name engraved on it. Or maybe he would receive a sand wedge studded with diamonds and jewels.

After several weeks, the postman knocked on the door of the golfer's house. He presented him with a small envelope that contained a certified letter. The golfer was a little confused. He had been anticipating a large package containing a valuable golf club. To his amazement, the golfer found a deed to a *five-hundred-acre* golf club with the letter. The golfer began to realize that kings think a little differently from the rest of us.

Just as the Saudi king had a different perspective about the value of the golf pro, we need to realize that God thinks differently from the way we do about our value and purpose. The King of Kings and the Lord of Lords wants us to enlarge the vision we have of ourselves and to see ourselves as he sees us. He wants to transform our thinking so that we rethink how we see ourselves. He doesn't want to give us small gifts but rather the biggest of all—his forgiveness, grace, and love. And he doesn't want us to waste our lives on petty goals. He wants to use us in the

> The King of Kings and the Lord of Lords wants us to enlarge the vision we have of ourselves and to see ourselves as he sees us

biggest, boldest, most important enterprise the world has ever known: impacting people's lives with the gospel of Jesus Christ so that they no longer conform but are transformed. There's no higher purpose.

We are capable because God has given us himself to empower us. Paul explained this important principle to the Philippians: "I have strength for all things in Christ Who empowers me [I am ready for anything and equal to anything through Him Who infuses inner strength into me; I am self-sufficient in Christ's sufficiency]" (Philippians 4:13 AMP). When I hear people doubt their capability to do what God asks of them, I think of the story of Moses. While Moses was tending a flock in the Midian wilderness, God appeared to him in a blazing fire from a bush. Miraculously, the bush wasn't consumed. In an awe-inspiring revelation of himself, God spoke to Moses and instructed him to go to Egypt to deliver the people of Israel from slavery. Feeling inadequate for this high calling, Moses responded by asking God, "Who am I, that I should go to Pharaoh and bring the Israelites out of Egypt?" (Exodus 3:11 NIV).

Does this sound familiar? It's often our response when God says we are valuable to him, and he wants us to make a difference in others' lives. We make our excuses just like Moses did: "O Lord, I have never been eloquent, neither in the past nor since you have spoken to your servant. I am slow of speech and tongue . . . Please send someone else to do it" (Exodus 4:10, 13). Moses saw himself as unworthy and ill-equipped to be used by God. But God saw something Moses didn't see. In Moses, God saw someone he had equipped for a specific task at a specific time to be done in a specific way. God was going to equip this eighty-year-old shepherd to lead a nation out of darkness into the light.

Take a minute to rethink your purpose and God-given skills:

- If an objective person looked at your life, what would he conclude is your compelling purpose in life?
- When have you helped people and experienced a deep sense of fulfillment? Are you still doing these things to love, care, and serve? Why or why not?
- What are the skills God has built into your life to make a difference in others' lives?

- How do you want God to use you to change people's lives in your office, neighborhood, home, or field?
- Do you dream God-sized dreams? How big are they? Do you expect to see these dreams materialize? Why or why not?

A LOOK IN THE MIRROR

When you're getting ready to go to work, to the club, to school, or out on the town, how do you know what you look like? You look in the mirror. Mirrors tell us about ourselves, but there are more kinds of mirrors than just the ones on the bathroom wall above the sink or behind the bedroom door. Every face we see each day is a mirror that reflects a message about our identity. From the time we're babies until today, the looks on the faces of our parents, siblings, friends, spouses, children, coworkers, and bosses give us powerful messages that shape our self-concepts. Too often, we see more frowns than smiles, and we only see smiles if we've done exactly what pleases those people. To win the smiles of the people we value, we become puppets on a string, living to please them by changing our behavior at the drop of a hat.

But there's another mirror, one that trumps all the rest. We need to look into the face of God to see that he smiles at us even when we're at our worst. He loves us unconditionally, and his steadfast love changes everything. That's what we've longed for. That's what we've wanted all our lives. When we are convinced that God loves us,

> When we are convinced that God loves us, we become secure and stable, confident but not cocky, humble but not timid.

we become secure and stable, confident but not cocky, humble but not timid.

How do we know what the face of God looks like? We look at Jesus Christ as he is described in the Bible. As the Creator, he simply spoke—and flung hundreds of billions of galaxies, each with hundreds of billions of stars, into the sky. His power and majesty are beyond anything we can imagine. But as the Savior, he tenderly touched a leper to heal him from his sickness and shame. On every page of the gospels, we see this incredible blend of power and gentleness. We don't gain a strong, secure identity by looking at ourselves; our hearts are filled only by looking at the One who loves us. He doesn't need anything or anyone, so his love is never manipulative. He loves simply because he delights to shower his people with affection. Even a taste of his greatness and goodness radically changes us from the inside out. There's nothing like it.

When we begin to develop a new, vibrant self-concept based on the grace of God, we long for him to use us in whatever way he chooses. As John Newton, the writer of the hymn "Amazing Grace," observed, we are available for God to use us—"whatever he wills, however he wills, whenever he wills." Instead of resisting God, being suspicious of his leading, or dragging our feet when we sense his nudge, we can't wait to join him in touching people's lives.

Fill your mind with the truth of God's Word, for it is the truth of God that will set you free and equip you to live a transformed life. To move in the right direction, start thinking different thoughts—positive, powerful, affirming thoughts about yourself and God's purpose for your life. As you fill your mind with the truth of God's Word, your sense of identity and security will soar. You will begin to realize that you are a child of the Most High God! And as you become more secure, you won't feel compelled to compete with others, to put them down so you can feel superior, or to hide from them out of fear. You'll want to live your life as God's beloved child and to follow his example of selflessly caring for others. You'll enjoy the delicious blend of freedom and the drive to make a difference. You no longer will feel like you have to conform to the world's ways. As a valuable, forgiven child of God, you have all the capabilities necessary to impact others for the glory of God.

Many of us fill our minds all day, every day, with destructive thoughts. They've become so common that we don't even recognize their destructive power. We spend countless hours nursing grievances instead of forgiving, thinking about what we want instead of being thankful for what we have, and feeling haunted by the past instead of being excited about the future. We call these "Really Awful Thoughts," or RATs.

> We spend countless hours nursing grievances instead of forgiving, thinking about what we want instead of being thankful for what we have, and feeling haunted by the past instead of being excited about the future.

A few years ago, I (Michelle) heard a sound that seemed to be coming from our attic. Rodney listened, and he heard it too. He assured me that it was just squirrels on the roof of the house. For days we heard the sound, but we didn't do anything about it. Finally, the consistency of the noise began to worry me. I called a pest control company, and their man set traps in our attic. A day or two later, he came back. When he climbed down the ladder, he was carrying a two-foot rat! It had been running around in our attic all that time, just a few feet away from our family!

Really awful thoughts are like that rat. If we don't recognize them and take action to get rid of them, they scurry around and thrive under our mental roofs. They won't go away if we don't know they're there, and they won't leave if we try to ignore them. They require a concerted effort to get rid of them.

We want to give you three principles and verses to focus on:

- God sees you as *valuable*. "You were bought with a price; do not become slaves of men" (1 Corinthians 7:23).
- God sees you as *forgivable*. "Just as He chose us in Him before the foundation of the world, that we would be holy and blameless before him" (Ephesians 1:4).
- God see you as *capable*. "I can do all things through Christ who strengthens me" (Philippians 4:13).

Some Christians have a misunderstanding of what Jesus meant when he told us, "Deny yourself, take up your cross, and follow me." He wasn't talking about having no identity, no self at all. In the Bible, the self refers to our sin nature. Jesus was telling us that if we want to follow him, we have to develop a habit of saying no to our selfish desires. The more we are changed by the grace of Jesus and amazed at his power, the more we'll want what he wants, and the more we'll become the people he wants us to be. The Danish theologian Søren Kierkegaard understood that following Christ enables us to find our true identities. He wrote, "Now, with God's help, I shall become myself."[4]

God wants you to transform your thinking. He has given you the *Word* of God, the *Spirit* of God, and the *people* of God to help you learn to rethink your self-concept and purpose. God has an incredible plan for your life. He sees you as capable and trustworthy to carry out his mission on earth. As you begin to think this way, be aware of resistant thoughts like the ones Moses had when God gave him

> God has an incredible plan for your life. He sees you as capable and trustworthy to carry out his mission on earth

a big vision. At that moment, don't run from him. Remember his love, his power, and his forgiveness, and put your hand in his.

There are two roads: one is broad, and the other is narrow. The broad road is a rat race of trying to create a self-image based on appearance, titles, possessions, and acceptance. Where has this road taken people? Where has it taken you? The narrow road doesn't have many people on it, but those who are there are learning to think by using a very different perspective—the truth of God's Word instead of the empty promises of our popular culture.

Are you on the narrow road now? It's the place to be.

Think about it . . .

Perspective

1. Describe (or perhaps show) others a photo from your past that you consider your least favorite. (It's okay to laugh at yourself!)
2. Why do you think the world places so much emphasis on physical appearance, possessions, or position in life?
3. How do you see yourself: as a valuable treasure or damaged goods, a masterpiece of God's creation or a disgusting castoff?

4. Read Isaiah 49:16. Where does God have your name written? Whose picture does he have constantly in front of him? How does that make you feel?

Choices

5. Identify three commercials, songs, or people who make you feel inadequate or "less than" in some way. What passage of Scripture will help you see yourself as valuable, forgiven, and capable?

6. The next time you feel haunted by guilt over things you've done, how will you cling to Christ's complete and loving forgiveness? When do you think your feelings of being forgiven will catch up to your faith that he has forgiven you?

Impact

7. Who are the people in your inner circle of influence? What impact are they having on you? What impact are you having on them?

8. What can you do today to help them (even just one of them) to believe he or she is valuable, forgiven, and capable?

CHAPTER 3

ReThink Happiness

Joy is not a distant destination at which you
arrive; rather it's a path you choose to
travel each day.
—Tommy Newberry

In *The Road Less Traveled*, Scott Peck begins the book
with a simple but profound statement: "Life is difficult."[5] I
(Rodney) used to think life was like hills and valleys. You
experience the difficulty and pain of a valley, and then you
climb up to enjoy the mountaintop—back and forth, an
endless cycle of ups and downs. I've realized, though, that a
better analogy for life is a set of railroad tracks with parallel
rails running the length of the line. These rails represent the
continuous presence of joys and heartaches, good times and
bad. Throughout our lives, we experience some wonderful
moments of love and joy, but we also suffer discouragements
and defeats—and we usually experience both happiness and
sorrow at the same time. If we don't accept the complexity
of life, we can develop unrealistic expectations. Then even
the little annoyances of life can rob us of happiness. Too
often we fall into a pattern of magnifying our problems—we
sweat the small stuff—and these minor challenges soon
capture our minds and become very big deals.

In many ways, people are a lot alike. In every generation
and every culture, people have had very similar values,
hopes, and fears. The biggest difference is found in our
attitudes—whether we see life as positive or negative. Our
perception of difficulties goes a long way to determine our
level of happiness. Do we see problems as stepping stones of
growth or straightjackets of bondage? Our view determines
everything about our purpose, our relationships, and,
ultimately, our happiness.

HAPPINESS IS A DECISION

When I (Michelle) was a little girl, my dad often came into my room in the mornings to wake me up with songs he called "happy songs." Sometimes he sang, "This is the day the Lord has made; we will rejoice and be glad in it" or "The joy of the Lord is my strength." During the day, he always kept the atmosphere positive around our houseful of girls. Whenever a catfight broke out, he would say, "Girls, do you know any happy songs you can sing?" This went on for years. No matter what happened, Dad was determined to teach us to have a positive outlook on life. (Actually, it became quite annoying. When you're a teenage girl with three sisters and in a bad mood, the last thing you want to do is sing a "happy song"!)

One day, Dad drove all of us to the airport in his new car. It was a beautiful car with light-grey cloth seats. We were rushing so that we wouldn't miss our plane. Mom and Dad were in the front, and all four girls were double-buckled in the back. I was running late getting ready that day, so I had taken my makeup bag into the backseat with me. As Dad drove, I attempted to put on my makeup—*liquid* makeup. Suddenly Dad hit a bump in the road, and my makeup flew out of the bottle and splattered all over me and my sisters—and all over Dad's beautiful new seats. Of course, one of my sisters immediately blew the whistle on me: "Dad, Michelle spilled her makeup!"

Dad was obviously frustrated. He said, "Michelle, I don't have time to stop. Just dust off your makeup onto the floor, and I'll clean it up later!"

My sister spoke up again. "But Dad, it's *liquid* makeup!"

Dad whipped the car over to the side of the road as fast as he could. He opened the back door and told me to get out. He then proceeded to try to wipe up dark-brown liquid with his bare hands and throw it out into the street. After a minute he said, "Michelle, get back in the car and just sit in it!" He was not happy!

After a few moments of cold silence in the car, my sister Kim spoke up. "Daddy?"

He said, "Kim, be quiet. I'm not in the mood to talk."

She said, "But Daddy?"

He barked, "Kim, don't you understand? I *do not* want to talk!"

But Kim wouldn't be quiet. She persisted, "But Daddy, I just have one question."

He grimaced. "Okay, Kim. What's your question?"

> Do you know any happy songs?

She smiled. "Daddy, do you know any happy songs?"

Dad couldn't help but smile.

Leadership expert John Maxwell observed, "Life is 10% what happens to me and 90% how I react to it." That's true for all of us. The adage, "Happiness is a decision you make, not an emotion you feel," is age-old wisdom we often need to rethink and apply.

> "Life is 10% what happens to me and 90% how I react to it."

In reality, we'll always have difficult challenges and negative circumstances. But in every situation, we have a choice: to let our circumstances sabotage us, steal our joy, or rob us of our happiness . . . or to trust in the goodness and greatness of God to use every situation for good in our lives.

Comparison and competition rob us of happiness. They cause us to focus on what we don't have instead of being thankful for all of God's blessings. German inventor Frederick Koenig observed, "We tend to forget that happiness doesn't come as a result of getting something we don't have, but rather of recognizing and appreciating what we do have."[6]

To rethink life's challenges, consider these questions:

- Do you consider yourself a happy person? Would others describe you as a person who sees life's glass as half-full or half-empty?
- On a daily basis, what recurring circumstances threaten to steal your happiness? On a larger scale, what struggles in life have significantly affected your happiness?
- Have you made the decision to be happy in life no matter what you face? If not, what difference would this commitment make?

One Sunday after our last morning church service, I (Michelle) walked out into the cafe and saw the beautiful, smiling face of my friend Karen. Along with a great group of women, she and I had been working hard for weeks to prepare for our first ReThink Pink women's conference. Karen had given hours of her time to raise funds and plan our silent auction to support a local battered-women's shelter. She and her family had recently gotten involved in church, and they were totally committed. As Karen and I talked that day, neither of us had any idea that, soon after she walked out the door, she would listen to a voicemail that would forever change her family's life.

Listening to her messages, Karen heard the voice of a Florida State Trooper say that her daughter Alisa had been involved in a serious car accident that morning and that she was in critical condition. The trooper said that Alisa had been airlifted to the hospital. Karen and John immediately jumped in their car and raced across town to find their daughter. She was in the ER, hanging on to life. When they arrived, they found that two of their daughter's best friends had lost their lives in the crash.

When Rodney and I heard the news, we got to the hospital as quickly as we could. We walked into a room full of devastated students trying to make sense of a senseless situation. We found our friends Karen and John. We were amazed at their composure and positive attitude in the midst of the hardest day of their lives. Karen immediately told me it was a blessing that a metal road sign had gone through Alisa's arm where it had. If it had been one inch over, it would have cut a main artery, and she probably would have bled to death. Karen told me how blessed they were to still have Alisa with them.

Karen's powerful, optimistic attitude continued for weeks as Alisa went through surgeries and rehab to help her begin to walk again. Karen's spirit was always positive. She talked often and always about the goodness of God and the lessons their family was learning. Of course, I assumed Karen wouldn't be available to help with the ReThink Pink Conference, because Alisa was scheduled to get out of rehab that week, and she would be in a wheelchair.

When I told Karen we'd miss her, she said, "Oh, Michelle, I'll be there. And Alisa wants to come and help too."

In a similar situation, most people would want to escape into their own world and dwell on their own pain and regrets, but Karen continued to reach out to help others. She and Alisa soon began another project: raising funds for seatbelt awareness.

Life is all about the attitude we have in the situations we've been dealt. I believe Alisa recovered so quickly because of God's graciousness in her life and because of the commitment by her parents and her to have a relentlessly positive attitude. In the darkest moment, Alisa, Karen, and John refused to give up or give in. They accepted the situation, opened their hearts to God, and learned some of life's most important lessons.

When we face difficulties, God wants us to make a choice—a conscious decision—to be happy, regardless of past, present, or future circumstances. Our goal should be to be genuinely happy individuals who find our peace and joy in our relationship with Christ. In his book, *Encouragement for Life*, author and pastor Chuck Swindoll observes, "We usually can do very little to change our lot. We can only change our reaction to our lot. We cannot change our past, for example. I don't care how brilliant we are, our past stands in concrete. We cannot delete it. But we can learn today to see our past from God's perspective, and use the disadvantages of yesterday in our life—today and forever."[7]

The apostle Paul understood this concept. Despite enormous trials in his life, including beatings, abandonment, physical illness, and countless life-threatening circumstances, he never allowed difficulties to steal his happiness. His late-in-life encounter with Christ changed his life, caused him to rethink everything, and led him to put his trust in God above any circumstances. But learning to be happy in every situation wasn't easy, even for this champion of the faith. He wrote the Christians in Philippi: "I have learned by now to be quite content, whatever my circumstances. I'm just as happy with little as with much, with much as with little. I found

> I found the recipe for being happy, whether full or hungry, hands full or hands empty, whatever I have, wherever I am, I can make it through anything in the one who makes me who I am.

the recipe for being happy, whether full or hungry, hands full or hands empty, whatever I have, wherever I am, I can make it through anything in the one who makes me who I am" (Philippians 4:11 MSG).

Paul wrote these words from prison. He had been arrested for preaching and teaching the gospel of Jesus Christ. He had been carried away to the city of Rome and put into a small prison cell—we would call it a dungeon. While Paul was in this cell, fighting and bickering broke out among some of the Christians in Rome. To make matters worse, some of them made it their goal in life to discredit Paul and his message about Jesus. To say the least, things weren't going well for Paul.

Many New Testament scholars believe that, to make matters worse, Rome's sewage system literally ran through the underground prison cells. When it backed up, the sewage could be up to a prisoner's waist. When Paul wrote these words, he wasn't only imprisoned unjustly, but he was potentially standing in waist-deep raw sewage. And if he ever got out, some people had pledged to murder him. Talk about a bad day! In this situation, Paul penned a letter to his brothers and sisters in Christ in Philippi—a church he had started years earlier on his travels—and shared his heart. Near the end of his letter, he explained that he had learned an important spiritual secret: to be content whatever his circumstances. If Paul could learn the secret of contentment in his circumstances, maybe you and I could learn it in ours. In *The Power of Determination*, author and speaker Joyce Meyer notes, "The key to happiness and fulfillment is not in changing our situation or circumstances, but in trusting God to be God in our life."[8]

HAPPINESS IS A PERSON

Many of us miss out on true joy and happiness in all circumstances of life—the good and bad, blessings and trials—because our expectations are still shaped by the values of our culture instead of the truth of God's Word. If all we have is the world's perception, we compare our lives with others and often feel "less than," and we compete with others, driving them away instead of loving them. We simply can't experience the contentment God intends for us apart from knowing Christ and gaining wisdom from him. Before Paul learned to experience happiness in his painful and difficult circumstances, he learned that true happiness is only found in a person—Jesus Christ.

The same is true in our lives. Only Jesus can bring us true happiness. He is the one who satisfies our deepest hungers and quenches our deepest thirst. He is the one who fills our hearts with the love we've always wanted. What we're looking for can't be found in pleasure, the applause of people, or any measure of success, but only in knowing and loving Jesus. It's an "inside job." On the night he was arrested, Jesus talked to his followers about putting God first in their lives because everything good comes from him. Then he explained, "I have told you this so that my joy may be in you and that your joy may be complete" (John 15:11 NIV).

> What we're looking for can't be found in pleasure, the applause of people, or any measure of success, but only in knowing and loving Jesus. It's an "inside job."

In the first chapter of Jesus's letter to the Philippians, we find Christ's name mentioned seventeen times. Paul's perceptions about life were saturated with thoughts about Jesus. He saw his own circumstances, even the most difficult ones, as opportunities God gave him to bring glory to Christ. Paul didn't delight in suffering. But he recognized that we all face challenging circumstances. In good times, we grow close to Christ out of gratitude. In tough times, we grow closer to him because we desperately need his love, strength, and guidance. In every circumstance, our lives are all about Jesus.

In difficult times, we can experience true happiness because we realize that our faithful and good God is at work in our lives. Every open door and every obstacle is an opportunity to show the world Christ's love and power. As we trust God, he gives us true inner peace and satisfaction unlike anything the world offers. Apart from God, nothing else truly matters. Paul explained, "But Christ has shown me that what I once thought was valuable is worthless. Nothing is as wonderful as knowing Christ Jesus my Lord. I have given up everything else and count it all as garbage . . . All I want is Christ and to know that I belong to him. All I want is to know Christ and the power that raised him to life" (Philippians 3:7-10 CEV).

To rethink the source of your happiness (and *un*happiness), ask yourself these questions:

- How do you define *happiness*? In your life, to what extent is it tied to pleasant circumstances?
- How has your relationship to Christ helped you experience happiness even in dark times?
- When going through difficult times, have you experienced God's presence and purpose? How is that different from what the world's values produce in people when they go through hard times? How did your experience shape the way you thought about God?

HAPPINESS IS A PROCESS

The goal of the Christian life isn't to achieve some superficial standard or to check off rules we've followed to earn God's approval. Like any relationship, our connection with God has meaning only when love grows deeper and trust becomes stronger. In the same letter to the Christians in Philippi, Paul explained, "Yes, everything else is worthless when compared with the infinite value of knowing Christ Jesus my Lord. For his sake I have discarded everything else, counting it all as garbage, so that I could gain Christ" (Philippians 3:8).

But Paul wasn't a narrow, rigid perfectionist. He was completely realistic about what it means for a finite human being to relate to an infinite God. He told them, "I don't mean to say that I have already achieved these things or that I have already reached perfection. But I press on to possess that perfection for which Christ Jesus first possessed me. No, dear brothers and sisters, I have not achieved it, but I focus on this one thing: Forgetting the past and looking forward to what lies ahead, I press on to reach the end of the race and receive the heavenly prize for which God, through Christ Jesus, is calling us" (Philippians 3:12-14).

> As we walk with Christ, the joy is in the journey, not the destination.

As we walk with Christ, the joy is in the journey, not the destination. The way we grow is by sticking with the process refusing to give up or give in when times are hard. *Growing* implies that we haven't arrived but that we're taking the steps we need to take to make progress. How do we grow? We can certainly grow stronger in our faith in good times, but we grow even more during times that test our faith and force us to think more deeply about God and his character. Satan and people may be trying to hurt us, but God uses every circumstance for good if we'll trust him.

When we work out at the gym with weights, the resistance produces muscle mass and strength. The same principle is true in our spiritual lives. The Bible describes us as "clay pots." If we're honest, we have to admit that we have cracks in our pots! Our imperfections reveal what is inside of us—faith and fear, hope and horror. If we try to deny our faults and failures, we fail to listen to God and learn the lessons he wants us to learn. But if we're honest about the pain in our lives, we learn to trust God more deeply than ever before.

Through the process, God is with us every step of the way, and his Word assures us that nothing can separate us from his love. No challenge or heartache will ever cause him to love us less. In every moment, he invites us to trust him. As we walk with him, he shapes us, purifies our motives, deepens our faith, and creates a heart of compassion for those who are going through similar difficulties. That's what it means to "be conformed to the image of Christ."

In countless experiences, Paul learned that God is faithful. He had seen God at work in his life in so many situations that he learned there was no time or reason to question God's faithfulness. He never allowed his circumstances to rob him of the joy he

> "And I am certain that God who began the good work within you will continue to work until it is finally finished on the day when Christ Jesus returns"

found in his relationship to Jesus Christ. Paul learned that genuine and lasting happiness is a decision we make, not an emotion we feel. He understood that true happiness is found in Christ. He wrote, "And I am certain that God who began the good work within you will continue to work until it is finally finished on the day when Christ Jesus returns" (Philippians 1:6).

We are all a work-in-progress. God's not finished with us. We shouldn't focus on past or current difficulties. Instead, we need to understand that God has us right where we are for a specific purpose. He wants to use adversity and blessing to equip us to reach a lost and hurting world. The apostle Paul realized that the suffering in his life was an opportunity to glorify Christ and to represent him so that other people could notice and trust in him. That's seeing things from an eternal perspective.

THE PROCESS OF CHANGE

To experience consistent joy, we need to put three principles into practice. Like learning to play a sport or a musical instrument, it takes practice to master these principles, but when we do, they become important habits of the heart.

1. Choose your thoughts.

We may not be able to control our feelings, but we can control our thoughts. We have the ability—and the responsibility—to notice what's going on between our ears and to decide to focus on truth that is good, right, noble, and encouraging. When we focus our thoughts on God's love, power, forgiveness, and faithfulness, our emotions will gradually come into line. If we want to

> The battle for our hearts is waged in our minds. It's not easy to change our thoughts, but it's crucial if we're going to learn to respond to every situation with faith and joy.

change the way we feel, we start by changing the way we think.

The battle for our hearts is waged in our minds. It's not easy to change our thoughts, but it's crucial if we're going to learn to respond to every situation with faith and joy. Paul wrote to the Corinthians about this battle. "We are human, but we don't wage war as humans do. We use God's mighty weapons, not worldly weapons, to knock down the strongholds of human reasoning and to destroy false arguments. We destroy every proud obstacle that keeps people from knowing God. We capture their rebellious thoughts and teach them to obey Christ" (2 Corinthians 10:3-5).

When we become aware of fear, arrogance, greed, bitterness, or apathy in our lives, we need to stop and ask, "What have I been thinking about? What thoughts have been shaping my attitude and feelings?" When we stop and analyze our thoughts, we may quickly realize that our negative, destructive thoughts have poisoned our goals and relationships.

Some of us may read this principle and conclude, "But that's just normal for me. I always think like this." Yes, but it can be different. If we aren't careful, we can allow our thoughts to drift toward things that are negative, full of self-pity and bitterness. When we realize that our minds are drifting this way, we need to make an adjustment. When my (Rodney's) car tires were out of alignment, the car drifted to the right. I fought it for a long time, but then I decided to do something to fix the problem. I took the car to a mechanic, and he realigned the front end of my car.

That's a picture of what right thinking can do for us when we're drifting spiritually and emotionally. When our minds are out of alignment—focused on negative news reports, economic problems, the latest gossip, unfulfilled expectations, or sensuous television programs—we develop destructive thinking. When we listen to our negative friends and their constant talk of gloom and doom, our attitude becomes sour too. It may be the norm to conform, but Paul reminds us to fight hard in our mental war. When we're winning, we experience more joy, gratitude, and hope. It's a fight, but it's one we can win.

One of the most important weapons in this fight is *thankfulness*. Take time to write down seven things for which you're grateful. They might be family members, your job, your health, friends, or other blessings God has given you. Post these where you can see them, and give thanks often for God's goodness to you.

We often let all kinds of negative, self-defeating thoughts rumble around in our minds without challenging them and replacing them with God's Word. One of the most helpful tools in this battle is a set of principles, truths, and sayings that remind us of what's good, right, and noble. We have the opportunity and the responsibility to determine what goes on in our minds every minute of every day. We can choose to focus on God's truths that inspire and transform us.

> We have the opportunity and the responsibility to determine what goes on in our minds every minute of every day.

For generations, believers have memorized passages of Scripture to help them think God's thoughts. Some people assume they can't memorize anything, but that's simply not true. We memorize phone numbers, song lyrics, recipes, software instructions, directions, and any number of other things. All it takes is a little time and attention. I (Rodney) want to share some of the passages that have meant the most in my life with Christ. They've enabled me to rethink my identity, my direction, my relationships, and my purpose when I face all kinds of situations. I've adapted some of these verses to make them personal.

"If God is for me, who can ever be against me"
(Romans 8:31).

"The Spirit who lives in me is greater than the spirit who lives in the world" (1 John 4:4).

"I can do everything through Christ who gives me strength" (Philippians 4:13).

"With God everything is possible"
(Matthew 19:26).

"The joy of the Lord is my strength"
(Nehemiah 8:10).

Write one of these verses on a card, and put it in your pocket. Read it a dozen times during the day. By the time you go to bed, you will have memorized it, and the truth of it will be changing how you think about every aspect of your life. In a few days, do the same thing with another verse. Soon you'll have a catalog of powerful verses riveted in your mind. This isn't magic; it's God's way of transforming you "into a new person by changing the way you think. Then you will learn to know God's will for you, which is good and pleasing and perfect" (Romans 12:2).

2. Enthusiastically embrace each day.
The second ingredient in a recipe for happiness is to practice living enthusiastically, one day at a time. When we add yesterday's failures and tomorrow's fears to the worries

of today, we can easily become overwhelmed. When we focus on the current day, we can maximize every moment, every relationship, every opportunity, and every challenge, and we'll live life to its fullest. Worrying about our past and fearing for our future destroys happiness in the present.

Past and future days are out of our control and in God's hands. One of the most important challenges in life is to figure out what we *can* control and, therefore, what we *can't*. Most people never get it right, so they worry about things they can't control. Jesus told his followers, "Seek the Kingdom of God above all else, and live righteously, and he will give you everything you need. So don't worry about tomorrow, for tomorrow will bring its own worries. Today's trouble is enough for today" (Matthew 6:33-34).

The word *worry* can mean "to choke or pull apart." When we moved to Florida, I (Rodney) noticed that a type of grass was taking over our front yard. After a week or so, a neighbor told me that it was a weed and it was choking out the good grass from our lawn. When we allow our minds to be overwhelmed with worry and to dwell on the things that are beyond our control, we begin to be pulled in all directions. The worries distract us, choking out the joy, happiness, and excitement of life.

When we focus only on the things we can control and trust God with the rest, we're free to live with unbounded enthusiasm. The word *enthusiasm* comes from two Greek words, "en" and "theos," which means "inspired by God." Our joy and happiness come from God, and our enthusiasm originates in him. That's exactly how we can live each day! There's no greater source of inspiration than God's Word. We can start our day by putting the Word of God into our minds and hearts so we can serve the Lord with enthusiasm, no matter what challenges come our way. Paul encourages us, "Serve the Lord enthusiastically" (Romans 12:11).

Rethink the way you're currently living. Are your facial expressions, attitude, and actions attractive to others? Do people see you enthusiastically and positively living your life? Be an inspiration to others—not for personal glory but to point others to your good and faithful God. My children have often found it amusing that total strangers begin talking to me (Michelle) as we stand in a line at the store, the bank, or anywhere else. They tell me their life stories just because I've looked them in the eye and given them a warm smile. If we live today like it might be our last, we're going to stand out.

3. Live every day trusting God.

We have a choice: We can trust our own abilities to make life work, or we can trust the God of the universe—the one who existed before time began, who created everything that exists, and who has proven his love for us in countless ways. So the question each of us must ask, every moment of the day, is this: *Who is more trustworthy, God or me?* Solomon, one of the wisest people who ever lived, wrote, "Trust God from the bottom of your heart, and don't try to figure out everything on your own" (Proverbs 3:5 MSG).

> We have a choice: we can trust our own abilities to make life work, or we can trust the God of the universe.

If you try to figure out everything on your own, it'll wear you down. If you attempt to take on the world's problems, it will zap the enthusiasm right out of you. To stop worrying and start trusting, we turn back to Paul's letter to the Philippians for advice. He instructed them, "Don't worry about anything, but pray about everything. With thankful hearts, offer up your prayers and requests to God. Then, because you belong to Christ Jesus, God will bless you with peace that no one can completely understand. And this peace will control the way you think and feel" (Philippians 4:6-7 CEV).

Sometimes difficulties challenge our faith in God. In our darkest times, we cling to what we knew about God when we walked in the light. Our confidence in God's character keeps us strong. Our friend Wilson Joseph was born in Haiti, the poorest country in the western hemisphere. When he was sixteen, he came to the United States. He graduated from high school and then worked his way through community college. While he was working as a manager at a restaurant, he fell in love with Tammy. They got married and had a daughter, but their growing family struggled because Wilson was also married to his career.

Several years later, he and Tammy were sleeping at home with their daughter Abigail and newborn son Jacob. They heard loud knocking on their door. Wilson ran to the door and asked, "Who is it?"

The voice insisted, "Open the door!"

Wilson asked, "What's the problem? There must be a mistake."

The man said, "We're with Immigration and Customs Enforcement. Open the door!"

Wilson opened the door, and the officers immediately took him from his family. He was stunned, and Tammy was shocked to find herself suddenly alone. Most of us can't imagine the horror and confusion of a situation like this.

After months of denied appeals, he was deported to Haiti. Tammy had hoped for Wilson's release. Now she felt devastated. The children weren't old enough to understand, but they sensed their mother's heartache.

Wilson hadn't been in Haiti for fifteen years, and he had few remaining roots there. He prayed often and hard for God to open a door for him to return to Tammy and the kids, but every door seemed closed.

For two years, Wilson and Tammy prayed, hoped, and waited. But all they heard was a deafening silence from the authorities. Wilson got involved in life-changing ministry. He started a prayer group with some men, and before long, the group had grown, and they led more men to Christ. Finally, after Wilson had lived for three years in Haiti, the authorities allowed Tammy and the children to come for a visit. It was a wonderful time, but it broke their hearts when it was time for them to leave.

When the earthquake devastated Haiti on January 12, 2010, Wilson and his friends looked for survivors, and they worked with relief organizations to provide care for orphans. Within two days of the disaster, Wilson and his friends were on the border of the Dominican Republic to join an American rescue team. Suddenly, God spoke to him and gave him insight about all the troubles he had experienced. During those long, painful years, he had asked God for wisdom and direction. Now he realized that God had answered those prayers and was revealing to him his greater purpose for being in Haiti.

Wilson and the team worked tirelessly to care for the quake victims. Their efforts and prayers resulted in developing a new ministry organization: Stepping Stone Haiti. They served more than 3,500 children in Carrefour and coordinated their efforts with a network of forty orphanages across Haiti. As Wilson cared for these children, his heart melted. He commented, "We realized that these precious kids in Haiti wanted nothing more than to be loved, cared for, and educated." God had placed him there for that very purpose.

A few months later, Tammy called to give him the good news that the immigration waiver had been approved, and he could come back to the United States. As always, the paperwork proved to be a hassle, but finally he received the approvals and was ready to return to the States.

As he and Tammy look back on those years, they see the strong, loving hand of God at work in their lives, even when they had no idea what he was doing. Wilson is especially grateful for the way the people from our church embraced and supported Tammy and the children while he was away. And he has a new appreciation for the mystery of God's will, his timing, and his divine purposes to use suffering for good. He reflected, "To me, God's faithfulness isn't what we get out of our relationship with him when we want it. It is doing his work when he calls us, and believing and trusting in the process."

Wilson and Tammy could have given up on God during the long ordeal and painful separation, but they refused to let their hope in God die. They suffered from confusion, heartache, and unreasonable delays, but they determined to trust God through it all. After they were reunited, they looked back and saw how God had been faithful, even in their darkness. They learned to trust God more deeply than ever—instead of blaming him for their troubles and vanishing into a pit of self-pity. They could have let their circumstances rob them of faith and steal their happiness, but they didn't. They chose faith, hope, and love, even in the middle of their heartache. They learned that they could experience real happiness anytime, anywhere.

Like Wilson, learn to see your challenges from God's perspective. Realize that your problems are pretty small when you compare them to the majesty, power, purposes, and wonder of Almighty God, who is fully capable of doing what you alone can't do. Fill your mind with the truth of his Word. Choose to be happy in spite of your circumstances, because happiness is a decision you make, not an emotion you feel. The broad road promises happiness but leaves us empty and confused. Only Christ's narrow road gives us genuine and sustained happiness. Are you on that road?

Think about it . . .

Perspective

1. Take a quarter and hold it with your arm stretched out in front of you. Notice that the quarter seems small when compared to your surroundings. When you move the quarter in, nearer to your eyes, it appears much larger. If fact, if you hold it close enough, you won't be able to see anything else. How does this exercise illustrate how worry affects our outlook? To what extent is this true in your life these days? Explain your answer.

2. Read Philippians 2:5. On a scale of 1 to 10 (1=bad; 10=great), how would you rate your current attitude toward your circumstances? Would your current attitude attract people to you and to Jesus Christ? Why or why not?

3. Whom do you know that best exemplifies what this chapter is about—a person who dwells on the goodness and greatness of God and who finds true happiness in virtually every circumstance? How has this person affected you?

Choices

4. What are seven things for which you're thankful? Take time to express your gratitude to God for them. Tell someone about one of them.
5. Review the three ingredients of the recipe for consistent happiness. Which of these do you need to focus on? What are specific steps you'll take to make them a habit in your life?

Impact

6. Who is the person most affected by your attitude? How would a more cheerful, optimistic, enthusiastic perspective on your part have a positive impact on that person?
7. Think about what's been going on in your mind in the past few days. What are your biggest worries? What truth from God's Word speaks most powerfully about this concern? Take time to think about it, meditate on it, and memorize this passage. How will a new surge of faith in God's goodness and power begin to dissolve your worries and replace them with faith?
8. Who are the people who will be most positively affected when you display an optimistic attitude, even in tough times? What difference will it make to them?

CHAPTER 4

ReThink Priorities

> There can be no happiness if the things we
> believe in are different from the things we do.
> —Freya Stark

Good intentions don't guarantee good results. When we walk away from God and mess up our lives, we're sure we deserve the natural consequences of heartache we experience. But when we try to do the *right* thing and things blow up, we're plagued with feelings of "should have" or "could have." Regret and disappointment color the way we remember our past: *I wish I'd done this or that. I wish I'd focused more on accomplishing good things instead of being absorbed in worthless things. I wasted so much time and resources doing that. My priorities were way off-base.*

Rethinking our lives is crucial if we want to make positive changes for the future, but we have to be careful to avoid getting stuck in the pain and disappointment of the past. Keeping our eyes fixed on life's rearview mirror is a tragic mistake that causes us to miss out on God's blessings in front of us. It's certainly possible to move beyond our past failures and poor decision-making. It's not

> Keeping our eyes fixed on life's rearview mirror is a tragic mistake that causes us to miss out on God's blessings in front of us.

only possible; it's also God's promise for his children. The "God of second chances" wants to rescue us from our past and do something fresh in our families, careers, finances, and futures. Renewing our purpose has always been God's plan. He spoke through Isaiah, saying, "I am going to do something new. It is already happening. Don't you recognize it? I will clear a way in the desert. I will make rivers on dry land" (Isaiah 43:19 GWT).

God is never surprised by anything that happens. He exists in eternity, outside time and space. He sees everything from beginning to end, and his plans are always good for his children. In fact, he's always in the process of doing something new. Though we may not recognize it, he has been working behind the scenes, allowing circumstances and people to get our attention, helping us focus on what matters most, and reprioritizing our lives.

Of course, we have a very limited perspective. We see only a tiny fraction of what God is doing behind the scenes. We're easily distracted, and we're often preoccupied. The noise of the world often drowns out God's voice as he speaks to our hearts. Over and over he whispers, "Pay attention. Don't miss out on my plans. I want to create a new life for you. I want to clear out a new path for you to get out of the dry land you've been experiencing—in your marriage, your relationship with your children, your financial world, your career—in the desert where you've been wandering. I want to take you to the banks of new rivers for your successful journey through those desert wastelands. I want to usher in something brand new in your world!"

Do you believe God is really good? Do you believe he has wonderful plans for you? In his most famous sermon, Jesus encouraged people not to give up when their dreams aren't fulfilled. He said, "Keep on asking, and you will receive what you ask for. Keep on seeking, and you will find. Keep on knocking, and the door will be opened to you. For everyone who asks, receives. Everyone who seeks, finds. And to everyone who knocks, the door will be opened" (Matthew 7:7-8).

To make sure they got the message, Jesus compared God's delight in giving gifts to us with a loving parent's desire to bless children. He connected the dots for them.

"You parents—if your children ask for a loaf of bread, do you give them a stone instead? Or if they ask for a fish, do you give them a snake? Of course not! So if you sinful people know how to give good gifts to your children, how much more will your heavenly Father give good gifts to those who ask him" (Matthew 7:9-11).

One of our problems in rethinking our priorities is that we so quickly give up on God's plans for us. We pray and we hope, but when the answer doesn't come quickly enough (or it's not the answer we wanted), we bail out. Our first priority, then, is to refocus our thoughts on the character of God and realize that he is completely trustworthy—even when he doesn't do exactly what we want him to do for us.

TWO COMMON MISTAKES

To experience the changes God wants to bring about in our lives, we need to turn up the volume on God's leading and stay in tune with his priorities. As we listen to him, we need to clearly separate ultimate priorities from daily commitments so we don't get bogged down in the mundane things of life. We need to keep first things first.

What are our priorities? How are they different for different people? When Jesus was asked about the most important commandment in the Old Testament, he replied that loving God with our whole heart and loving people were the summation of the hundreds of specific commands in the Bible. Those, he said, are our ultimate priorities. But the way we live those out may not look the same for any two people.

First, let's rethink our priorities by answering a few questions:

- What are your top five priorities in life?
- If an objective person watched you for a week, what would he or she conclude are your priorities?
- The way we use time and money reflects our true priorities. List your five most significant time commitments in an average week. List five most important financial commitments in an average month.
- How do these time and money commitments line up with your stated priorities?

When people ask us about our priorities, we may respond by identifying key relationships—with God, spouses, children, family, friends, church family—as most important. Foremost in our commitments may be our work—our employment, our career outside the home—because it demands so much of our time and energy, often competing with our marriage, family, or other important relationships. Outside of our work, we have many other commitments, including time with friends, relaxation, and hobbies and recreation—things like golf, tennis, basketball, camping, fishing, hunting, Facebook, the Internet, television, music, and movies. Then we have our toys—our boat, motorcycle, bicycle, lake house, beach condo, guns, and mountain cabin. If we have kids, we're dedicated to going to their events—gymnastics, dance, cheerleading, baseball, soccer, basketball, football, track events, music lessons, scouting programs, and school events. The list of commitments can seem endless.

When we look at this list, we may think, *Whoa, man, I'm maxed out! I've got a lot going on in my life.* And for many of us, it's true. We're rushing around so much, doing the *pressing* things, that we've forgotten to rethink life to be sure we're doing the *crucial* things. We're overwhelmed by all the stuff we have to do, places we have to be, and people we have to please. We never seem to have any white space on our calendars—no time for ourselves, no time to relax, and no margin to just chill. The never-completed list of things-to-do haunts us—the chores that never get done, the homework, the housework, the yard work, and volunteering to help others. Many of us are so tired that we're on the edge of burn out. And some of us are over the edge.

Friends, this isn't the abundant life God promised! Rethinking our lives calls for a rigorous analysis and adjustment of our commitments. Do they line up with our priorities? Do our commitments work in sync with the things we claim to be most important in our lives?

Rethinking our lives calls for a rigorous analysis and adjustment of our commitments. Do they line up with our priorities?

Our commitments often take precedence in our lives and compete with our priorities. These time-consuming, energy-draining commitments can eclipse those things that are so incredibly important. We need to recognize the two mistakes we often make when we try to sort out how we should be spending our days, resources, and affections.

Mistake Number One: We misjudge the distance between our priorities and commitments.

On one of our visits with family in Texas, we stayed at Michelle's sister's home. The last night of our visit, we packed our bags so we could leave early the next morning for our flight back to Orlando. I (Rodney) didn't sleep well that night, because I anticipated the stress and strain of getting the kids up and dressed so we could be out the door by 4:30 a.m.

In the early morning darkness, I got up, dressed, and started to load the car. To make as little noise as possible, I was barefoot. I started carrying several enormous suitcases down the winding staircase to the front door. In the pitch-black darkness, I misjudged the last step, where the surface changed from carpet to hardwood. I slipped, landed on my big toe, and sent suitcases flying through the air! I was in some serious pain. I probably broke my toe. (To this day that toe doglegs to the right and hurts in cold weather.)

My mishap reminds me of what can happen when we misjudge the distance between our commitments and priorities. It can create a lot of pain and frustration. It can also cause us to lose sight of what's most important, make dumb choices, and consume a lot of time as we try to remedy a bad situation we've caused. No wonder we're so frustrated and stressed! Many of us are overcommitted. We've said yes to so much that we feel powerless to do the things we really want to do, to spend quality time with those we love and to enjoy the transformed life God wants for us. Why do we keep doing this to ourselves? Because we continually misjudge the distance between our commitments and priorities.

Mistake Number Two: We fail to see the importance of the seemingly insignificant.

Many of our commitments—coaching Little League, PTA, hobbies, caring for an elderly relative, volunteering, and on and on—are good things. Each one may be a wonderful cause, a worthwhile activity, or the perfect pastime. But here's the issue: collectively, they may be too much for us to handle.

Most of us are busy people who tend to say yes to too many good things. We think accepting one more obligation is no big deal. We assume we can juggle an additional short-term commitment or squeeze in a little more fun. We're confident we'll adapt to the new commitment. After all, it's just a small thing. Oh, our stress level may go up for a while, but we expect that. In a week or two, we're sure the current craziness will eventually ease off. Things will settle down so we can handle everything. No problem.

Wrong! Like the proverbial frog in a kettle, the heat of additional commitments slowly rises until we're cooked! We want to make a change, but we believe we're locked in to the new commitments with no way out. And some of us fail to learn anything from repeated mistakes of overcommitment. We keep jumping back into the hot water, saying yes to everything that comes along. When we think of saying no for a change, we feel guilty, or fear someone will ask what's wrong with us. We don't want to feel left out or that we've let anyone down, so we bravely nod that we're in again.

To be sure, any one or two of these commitments is perfectly good and right, but the cumulative effect can be devastating. We simply must learn to set priorities and live by them. We have to rethink how we're investing our lives

> Saying yes to too many good things causes us to miss out on the best things God has in store for us.

so we can make a difference for God. Saying yes to too many good things causes us to miss out on the best things God has in store for us. Seminary professor Dr. Howard

Hendricks accurately noted, "The secret of concentration is elimination."[9]

Samson—the Bible's bodybuilder and an incredibly strong man—is a good example of how even the most devoted believers can miss out on God's best by allowing themselves to be compromised by little things. God had an important plan for Samson's life. He was born to parents who had been childless for many years. After praying for a long time to have a child, an angel of the Lord appeared and told them they would soon have a son who would do mighty things for the children of Israel. These parents were instructed to raise Samson to be totally dedicated to God under a Nazarite vow (Judges 13:5). To be raised as a Nazarite meant that Samson made three vows: never to eat or drink any grapes or its products (raisins, wine, or any fermented drink), never to touch anything dead, and never to cut his hair (the secret of his strength). Samson grew to be a man with awesome physical strength. He single-handedly won battles against the Philistines. Samson had a specific purpose that God wanted to fulfill in his life. God was going to use this giant of a man—but not just his natural strength. The Spirit of the Lord would supernaturally empower him to defend the children of Israel and its army. Because of Samson, Israel enjoyed peace in the Promised Land.

Even though God tremendously blessed and used him to accomplish great things, Samson was unable to keep his vows. In fact, the Bible records that he broke all three. Samson's story begins with his marriage to a Philistine woman, despite his parents' protests that it was a violation of God's law. To obtain his new bride, he and his parents traveled through the lush vineyards of Timnah, where a lion attacked Samson. With his bare hands, he fought and killed the lion. Not long after this, he saw that bees had created a honeycomb in the carcass of the lion. Because Samson had a sweet tooth, he reached inside the dead animal and got some of the honey. He must have thought, *This is an insignificant thing. It's no big deal. Surely breaking the Nazarite vow one time won't hurt anything.*

Later, at his bachelor party before his wedding, Samson partied hard one last time. The feast was a drinking bash. In this wild and drunken environment, he was tempted to sin. He probably thought it was another insignificant thing, but this seemingly small compromise led to Samson murdering thirty Philistine men.

At this point, Samson had broken two of his three Nazarite vows and sinned against God, but God continued to use him to accomplish his purpose: to begin "the deliverance of Israel from the hands of the Philistines" (Judges 13:5). In light of God's amazing grace to keep using this flawed man, we might think that Samson would have responded in gratitude and obedience to God when given another chance. Instead, Samson broke the third part of the Nazarite law: no haircut. How did this happen?

The "he-man" Samson had a "she" problem: a weakness for beautiful women. The Bible tells us he was enticed by a Philistine prostitute named Delilah. Night after night, he visited her, and he fell madly in love with her. She seduced him and convinced him to reveal the secret of his strength. Eventually he gave in and shared the secret. As a result, she got him drunk and had her countrymen cut his hair while he was asleep with his head in her lap. As a result, he lost his strength.

At every point in Samson's decline into sin, shame, and weakness, Samson rationalized his choices, but each poor decision became enormously significant in his life. He lost his power, was blinded and bound in prison shackles, and never experienced many of the blessings of God. Even though he repented and made things right with God, his life and service had been destroyed.

In my (Rodney's) role as a pastor, I often hear stories of lives and marriages destroyed by seemingly insignificant choices. These people often started out doing good but ultimately self-destructed because rationalized, bad decisions took their devastating toll on them. Misguided priorities and selfish desires distracted them from seeking God and his best plan for their lives. The boat, the condo, the promotion, and all the toys eventually shackled these people in a debt-prison of their own making. Instead of enjoying lives full of potential and true joy, they're tormented by poor choices, financial disasters, sexual indiscretions, and strained and broken relationships. When people misjudge the distance between their commitments and their priorities, the seemingly insignificant becomes very significant. Johann von Goethe knew something about priorities. He was a German artist, writer, and physicist—one of the most gifted geniuses of his day. He wrote, "Things which matter most should never be at the mercy of things which matter least."

> "Things which matter most should never be at the mercy of things which matter least."

SAY NO TO THE GOOD AND YES TO THE BEST

If I were Satan, I know what I'd do: My number-one strategy to destroy people's lives, marriages, families, finances, careers, and relationships—all the things that matter—would be to make all of the good things in life overwhelmingly attractive. I would do everything I could to entice people to make commitments to do all these good things. There's nothing wrong with them, is there?

After observing people from all parts of the country, I'd say Satan has played these cards very shrewdly. Many people are so preoccupied with all the good things in life—thinking about them, acquiring them, showing them off, protecting them, and replacing them—that they don't have much time or attention for higher priorities. But most of us talk a good game. We say we love God and people, and we show up at church and Bible studies often enough to impress the people around us (and maybe even ourselves).

But there's a huge chasm between what we say is most important and how we spend our time, energy, affections, and money. Sooner or later, many of us wake up one day, see all the stress in our lives, and wonder: *How did I get here? Why do I keep making so many commitments? Why am I so tired—and so empty? How am I going to manage all these things? My life has gotten so complicated and cluttered!* When this happens, we begin to feel more dead than alive. All this stuff has robbed us of the things we treasure. In the past, we promised we'd never compromise, but we made a few choices that snowballed into the calamity of a stressed and empty life. Satan has done his job. Jesus told us, "The thief's purpose is to steal and kill and destroy" (John 10:10).

Rethink the good things in your life by answering these questions:

- Do your possessions and your desire for more cause problems in your life and in your relationships? If so, what are some of these stresses and strains?

- Do some of your commitments keep you from spending time with those you love, including your spouse, your children, and God?
- Would you categorize your life as being simple or complex? If it's complex, how complex is it?

A couple in our church has four very active children. We've been impressed as we've watched these parents make it a priority every week to get their kids to one of our weekend services—in spite of baseball tournaments, football games, basketball games, and cheer competitions. They make worship a priority for their family, even if it means driving a long distance after a game to come to the Sunday night service, or getting up early to go to the first service in order to get out on the field by eleven a.m. Other parents have seen their commitment as a little extreme, but there's no question in the kids' minds about their parents' priorities. They know that God is first in their family's life.

Over the years, Rodney and I (Michelle) have had to make some hard decisions concerning our priorities. In spite of a host of competing commitments, we've made it a priority for our family to have dinner together. Early in our marriage, we decided we would try to have a consistent date night. It was easy at first, but by the time we had three children in high school, middle school, and elementary school, it was quite a challenge! Making our date night a priority seems odd to some of our friends, but we're making investments in our marriage. If our marriage is strong, our kids, our friends, and our church will benefit too.

In addition, we've made a commitment to spend time with our kids at least one weekend night each week. This priority was modeled for me by my parents, and it's the reason my sisters are my best friends. Carving out a night to be together takes some adjustment at first—and a strong commitment when the kids are busy in middle school and high school. Our kids have had to say no to a lot of good things, but we believe our investment of time with them is the best for all of us.

Our homes shouldn't add to the stresses in our lives. We need to create a home environment that is a haven of love, peace, and joy—a place where our spouse and children find and follow God's priorities for their lives. In her book, *Disciplines of the Beautiful Woman,* Anne Ortlund wrote, "I believe that a godly home is a foretaste of heaven. Our homes, imperfect as they are, must be a haven from the chaos outside. They should be a reflection of our eternal home, where troubled souls find peace, wary hearts find rest, hungry bodies find refreshment, lonely pilgrims find communion, and wounded spirits find compassion."[10]

> Our homes, imperfect as they are, must be a haven from the chaos outside.

Good things, like our cell phones or computers, can become sources of stress. When we're on the edge of burnout, we can be pushed over the edge by something as simple as a ballgame, bake sale, or appointment. Add traffic jams, a sick child, plumbing problems, an overdrawn bank account, and work deadlines to the mound of stuff we have to manage, and it's easy to see why we have such a hard time focusing on the priorities God has given us. When the pressure builds, we eventually implode or explode. Tempers flair, and then joy and satisfaction are hard to find.

What can we do to turn the valve and lower the pressure? How do we make our commitments align with our priorities? We need to begin saying no to *many* good things, but not *all* good things. The good things in our lives aren't evil, but letting too many of them crowd out the most important things produces heartache. When our priorities are clear and strong, we can then make better choices about our daily and weekly commitments. We aren't driven and tossed by every demand and request. We have with wisdom to choose only the things that take us down the narrow road of God's good and perfect will for our lives. Then we experience far more peace, space to breathe, room to function, and freedom to enjoy God's gifts.

How do we get there? We begin by studying God's instruction manual to uncover his perspective of our priorities. Quite often this study reveals some things that are out of alignment, so we need to make adjustments. At this critical moment, we can either walk away from God's path or submit to him, his goodness, and his wisdom. Submission to God isn't a prison we want to escape at all costs. Just the opposite. We realize that he's the sovereign King and gracious Savior who has proven he is supremely trustworthy. When we get a glimpse of his character, we gladly submit to him. But it's always our choice. James, the half-brother of Jesus, wrote, "Submit yourselves, then, to God. Resist the devil, and he will flee from you. Come near to God and he will come near to you" (James 4:7-8).

Rethinking our priorities is a battle. Satan, the enemy of our souls, is at work to deceive, tempt, and accuse us to get us offtrack. But if we submit to God and resist the Devil, he'll back off. And as we come near to God, our Lord will come close to us and guide us so that we experience the fullness of life he intended. When we draw near to God, we'll be able to hear his guiding voice over the noise of the world. We make God our number-one priority, and we begin to live a lifestyle of worship. It's not just on Sunday morning for an hour; we find him worthy of our love and loyalty all day, every day.

Gradually we clean out the clutter in the center of our hearts. We replace misguided desires and compulsive behaviors with the love and truth of Jesus Christ. He becomes the driving force in our lives, our true priority. Life becomes an ongoing opportunity to enjoy him. Paul described this battle in his letter to the Christians in Corinth. He wrote, "But I fear that somehow your pure and undivided devotion to Christ will be corrupted, just as Eve was deceived by the cunning ways of the serpent" (2 Corinthians 11:3). It's easy to let our "pure and undivided devotion to Christ" become poisoned. That's Satan's goal for us, every minute of every day. The good news is that God has given us his wisdom to guide us and his power to strengthen us on the narrow road. We can experience victory in our battles.

To fight well, we need to establish clear priorities. We can illustrate these priorities with a glass jar, a handful of big rocks, and a large amount of pebbles and sand. If you fill the jar with the pebbles and sand—the small stuff—it will take up a lot of space in the jar and leave little room for the big stuff. The rocks won't fit. But if you prioritize and put the big rocks in first, you can still put a bunch of little pebbles in the jar too. Many of us make a big mistake. We spend all our time on the little things, and then we have no room in our schedules (or our hearts) for loving God and loving people. This can change. We must first make room in our lives for God and his plan for our lives. Then we can see which smaller things also fit.

Having the right priorities starts with being in agreement with God's heart and his plan. Our priorities are to come from God's principles, which are found in his Word. When our priorities conform to God's, our commitment of time, effort, and other resources follows logically. The first part of the word *priorities* is "prior." Our planning begins with prior, advanced decision-making. The non-negotiables of life are clearly spelled out in God's word. They're not a mystery. They're crystal-clear.

> Having the right priorities starts with being in agreement with God's heart and his plan. Our priorities are to come from God's principles, which are found in his Word.

LIVING IT OUT

After we submit to God's priorities, we make a commitment to live them out each day. God's word instructs us: "So watch your step. Use your head. Make the most of every chance you get. These are desperate times. Don't live carelessly, unthinkingly. Make sure you understand what the Master wants" (Ephesians 5:15-17 MSG). What does the Master want? Jesus told us, "My purpose is to give them a rich and satisfying life" (John 10:10).

To live according to God's priorities, we have to watch our step and use our head. We can't afford to live carelessly; the stakes are too high, and the battle is too fierce. We need to be tough-minded but tenderhearted. We have to be shrewd and analytical, reflecting on our purchases so we don't buy things just to keep up with a friend. We can't let our kids run crazy just because one of their friends' parents has no boundaries. And here's one you may not have expected to read in this book: we can't agree to be involved in every serving opportunity just because there's a need and someone asks us to volunteer. We need to exercise more wisdom in making choices, even choices about helping out at church. Seeking God in all things—financial decisions, purchases, habits, career, personal, and family matters—is essential if we want to enjoy the rich and satisfying life the Lord wants to give us. Here is a tip someone passed along to us years ago. Your availability should not be the reason why you say "yes" to things. Instead, we should make our decisions to say "yes" or "no" based upon wisdom not our availability.

> Your availability should not be the reason why you say "yes" to things. Instead, we should make our decisions to say "yes" or "no" based upon wisdom not our availability.

Proverbs 17:24 (TEV) *An intelligent person aims at wise action, but a fool starts off in many directions.* If we're not careful, we can find ourselves confusing activity with accomplishment.

Rethink how you've chosen to live out your priorities.

- How do you integrate your faith with daily life?
- What impact do God's priorities have on your decision-making? What are some ways you depend on God's Word for direction? How has God given you direction as you've prayed, listened to the Spirit's whisper, and felt his nudge?
- As you've followed Jesus, how has he been changing your desires and priorities?

MAKING A DENT

Following Christ means that we learn to value what he values, care the way he cares, and serve the way he served. The more we experience the life-transforming love of God and know we're forgiven and secure in his grace, the more we'll want to share his story with everyone who will listen, and we'll want to step in to meet all kinds of needs. That's what Jesus did, and that's what we'll want to do too.

Serving others will become a natural—actually, a *super*natural—expression of our connection to Christ and our sincere love for people. We'll look for ways to serve our spouse, children, friends, coworkers, and others—in the body of Christ, the community, and beyond. Our love for Jesus will spill out in a genuine passion to make a difference in people's lives.

One of the facts of Christianity in America is that, as many of us grow in our faith and our commitment to a church, we lose touch with unbelievers. We have new Christian friends, and gradually our skeptical buddies fall out of our circle. We don't intend for it to happen. It just does. For God's sake, and for the sake of the people in our communities, we need to intentionally put ourselves in a position to reach those who do not have a relationship with Christ and may not know any committed believers.

I (Rodney) go where the unchurched people hang out. I go with the purpose of making an impact, and God often gives me a chance to share Christ with others who are struggling with life. As I engage them in conversations about things they're interested in talking about, the discussion inevitably turns to Christ. They want to know how I and other Christians experience real peace in the midst of all the chaos.

When we take the initiative to step into the worlds of other people, we have the opportunity to explain how Jesus has transformed our lives, given us room in our lives to enjoy life, and provided freedom in our finances because we've listened to

> It's our privilege to represent him, and it's our responsibility to represent him well.

his direction and honored him with our financial resources. Because we are living out the priorities of our lives, we've narrowed the gap between our commitments and what truly matters most.

Jesus often used the metaphors of lights and lamps. In his day, that was the only way to see in a dark home or on a path at night. He explained that all of us are to be light in the dark world of our neighbors, family members, and friends. It's our privilege to represent him, and it's our responsibility to represent him well. Jesus told the crowd listening to him, "You're here to be light, bringing out the God-colors in the world. God is not a secret to be kept. We're going public with this, as public as a city on a hill. If I make you light-bearers, you don't think I'm going to hide you under a bucket, do you? I'm putting you on a light stand. Now that I've put you there on a hilltop, on a light stand—shine! Keep open house; be generous with your lives. By opening up to others, you'll prompt people to open up with God, this generous Father in heaven" (Matthew 5:14-16 MSG).

When we connect with others and serve them gladly, we will be a bright light to the people around us. We will radiate the love of God to our coworkers or classmates, those at soccer or cheerleading, our friends and family, believers and skeptics. What an honor! What a privilege!

Think about it . . .

Perspective

1. What are some ways a person can tell what his real priorities are?

2. How do your daily time and financial commitments support your priorities? How do they detract from them?

3. What is the difference between gladly submitting to God and submitting out of fear or guilt? Which of these best represents your reason to submit (or your resistance to submit) to God?

4. According to John 10:10, Jesus said that committing our life to God's priorities allows us to experience significant benefits. What are some of these?

5. What are some very practical, specific ways that Satan tries to keep us from lining up with God's priorities?

Choices

6. What are some of God's priorities to which you need to say yes?

7. What are some good things that have crammed your life too full, things that you need to say no to?

8. What difference will it make if you rethink your priorities and make real changes?

Impact

9. Read Matthew 5:14-16. What does it mean for you to be a light to the people around you?

10. What is one thing you can do today to be that light?

05

CHAPTER 5

ReThink Choices

> While we are free to choose our actions, we are
> not free to choose the consequences
> of our actions.
> —Stephen R. Covey

In October of 2001, Steve Jobs forever changed the course of media and entertainment distribution when he unveiled his creation, the Apple iPod. When this new device was launched, digital cameras, camcorders, and organizers were already established in mainstream markets. But Steve Jobs began to rethink these devices. He and his team found existing digital music players to be "big and clunky or small and useless" with user interfaces that were "unbelievably awful,"[11] so they decided to develop their own. Jobs ordered Apple's hardware engineering team to develop a device with a five-gigabyte hard drive. They produced the iPod First Generation, which put "1000 songs in your pocket."[12] After eight months of development, the iPod was announced to the world. The product shocked the computer industry, but in those early days, few people grasped the impact the iPod would have on the music industry and other media.

In rethinking MP3 players, Steve Jobs realized that companies in the music business, and even his own company, were focusing primarily on the device itself. He made the decision to shift a lot of the attention to the earbuds attached to his device. In their ads and on their gift cards, Apple marketed the iPod with a darkened silhouette of an individual dancing, holding an iPod, with white earbuds prominently dangling from the ears. Soon people began to associate the earbuds with the freedom and convenience of listening to thousands of songs. Steve Jobs and his team at Apple were geniuses at inventing new devices, but they were also brilliant at marketing those devices. Since October

2004, the iconic iPod line has dominated the sales of digital music players in the United States, with over 90 percent of the market for hard-drive-based players and over 70 percent of all types of players.[13]

Just as the iPod is usually hidden in a person's pocket, our hearts are often hidden too. No one can really see our hearts, but they can know our hearts by seeing the choices and decisions we make. Our choices advertise who we are—our values, our priorities, and the God we follow. People judge us by what they see us do and say. The choices we make reveal our character, the real "us," who we are on the inside. Solomon wrote, "As water reflects the face, so one's life reflects the heart" (Proverbs 27:19).

> No one can really see our hearts, but they can know our hearts by seeing the choices and decisions we make.

Values and choices are cyclical. Our values shape our daily choices, and our choices then reinforce or erode our stated values. For instance, if our highest goal in life is climbing the corporate ladder and making as much money as possible, we'll choose to step on and over people instead of loving them. When we get the promotion we've longed for, we feel powerful and superior, which confirms our values and compels us to repeat those choices, using people instead of loving them.

But this isn't the way God created the world to be! This pattern continues until the law of natural consequences catches up to us. Sooner or later, we reap a harvest of broken relationships, intense stress, and fatigue. At that point, we have the opportunity to look at our values, rethink what's important to us, and make different choices about our families, our careers, our friendships, and our sanity.

In the same way, when our chief desire in life is to know, love, and please God, we make choices each day that reinforce this supreme value. We carve out time to spend in the Bible and in prayer, we look for opportunities to help people around us, and we learn to see every obstacle as a stepping stone of growth, instead of a threat to our security. When people watch us making good and godly choices, some of them applaud, but some think we've lost our minds! We've stopped conforming to the world's way. We've chosen to get off the broad road that leads to destruction, and we've set foot on the narrow road that leads to life, peace, love, and joy.

If we say we're Christians but our choices don't reflect this new set of values and lifestyle, something's very wrong. We're either not really believers after all, or the lights haven't come on in our spiritual lives. Even people who are new to the faith and have truly grasped the life-changing grace of God realize that everything is different. Paul told the Corinthians that rethinking Christ, life, and our values radically alters our lives. He wrote, "So we have stopped evaluating others from a human point of view. At one time we thought of Christ merely from a human point of view. How differently we know him now! This means that anyone who belongs to Christ has become a new person. The old life is gone; a new life has begun!" (2 Corinthians 5:16-17).

Our choices matter. They reflect what we really believe, and they take us another step down the road—either the road that leads to more destruction or the road that leads to life. We need a grid "filter" to evaluate our choices. Let's look at some questions that help us rethink every decision we make.

IS THE CHOICE BASED ON TRUTH?

Our thoughts are the individual threads that make up the fabric of our lives, but we rarely stop to look carefully to see if there are any hidden motives and meaning in the things rattling around between our ears. Sometimes we can be surprised by what we find.

A few years ago I (Rodney) climbed up on the roof of our house to clean out the gutters. There was a particular place between the overhang of the roof and the upslope of the roof of the screened-in porch where a lot of leaves had accumulated. It had rained recently, and the mass of leaves was very thick and heavy. I was struggling to rake them away from the house. I stood on the edge of the roof and strained to pull the leaves between my legs. It was very awkward, but soon I had a huge pile.

Suddenly a furry head popped up at my feet! It was a big raccoon! It scrambled to the edge of the roof, but before it scampered away, it looked back as if to say, "Hey, mister! What do you think you're doing?" I was asking myself the same question. I had no idea that guy had been hidden in the pile of leaves.

The meaning and motives of our thoughts often remain hidden. No one gets up in the morning and determines, "Today I'm going to base my life on meaningless ideas and lies." We all believe that our perceptions are accurate. Because we are human and our thinking may be flawed, we need to take a long, hard look at the validity of the thoughts in our minds. King David gave us an example when he prayed, "Search me, O God, and know my heart; test me and know my anxious thoughts. Point out anything in me that offends you, and lead me along the path of everlasting life" (Psalm 139:23-24).

When we stop long enough to analyze our thoughts, we can ask: Are my choices based on peer pressure, convenience, or God's truth in the Bible? Earlier, we looked at Paul's explanation of what it means to surrender our lives to God in response to all of his mercies. The Christian life, though, requires tenacious discipline. Paul explained that it's essential that we change the way we think: "Don't copy the behavior and customs of this world, but let God transform you into a new person by changing the way you think. Then you will learn to know God's will for you, which is good and pleasing and perfect" (Romans 12:2).

How much are we listening to *God's truth* and letting it guide our choices, and how much are we letting *the world's* values press us into its mold? God loves us and wants what's best for us. His Word gives us principles to protect us—not to harm us. The truths of the Bible reflect his nature and character. On the narrow road, the Bible serves as fuel and guardrails. If you want to know God's will, get to know God's Word. His Word is the basis for all our choices.

> God loves us and wants what's best for us. His Word gives us principles to protect us—not to harm us.

God's grace has set us free, but we need to use our freedom for good. Paul wrote the Corinthians, "'Everything is permissible for me'—but not everything is beneficial. 'Everything is permissible for me'—but I will not be mastered by anything" (1 Corinthians 6:12 NIV). People often ask me about how close they can come to particular sins without getting on the wrong side of God.

I've often told teenagers, "If pre-marital sex is wrong, don't you think it would be wise to avoid the situations that lead to it? And if getting drunk is wrong, wouldn't it be wise to avoid the places and people who tempt you to drink and or get drunk?" I've asked married people, "If adultery is sin, don't you think it would be wise to avoid putting yourself in intimate conversations with people of the opposite sex?"

You get the point: Everything may be permissible, but not everything is beneficial. A wise person doesn't try to get as close as possible to the guardrail on a dangerous mountain highway. He stays far away on the other side of the road! All of us face "gray areas" that don't have clear-cut, black-and-white answers to the cultural and moral issues that confront us daily. When you face these situations, ask yourself these three questions:

1. What purpose does it serve?

Paul didn't want anything to get in the way of his fulfilling God's purpose for his life. Some places, people, and situations don't contribute to our spiritual vitality or help us take steps down the narrow road. (See 1 Corinthians 9:24-27 and Hebrews 12:1-2.) At the end of the day, how does this choice help me fulfill God's plan and purpose for my life?

2. Is it a good example or witness to others?

Paul never wanted his actions or decisions to be a stumbling block for others. (See Romans 14:13.) We don't ever want to put ourselves in a position that would send the wrong message to others.

3. Does it give me a clear conscience?

We can never go wrong by taking the narrow road. (See Psalm 18:23-24.) One of the blessings God gives us is a clear conscience so we can sleep peacefully at night.

We should live in a way that God applauds so that he will ultimately say to us, "Well done!"

Too often we hear media stories about celebrities who make poor life choices and face the humiliating consequences of their decisions. From outward appearance, these individuals seem to have everything going their way, but their conduct reveals character flaws that have been kept hidden from the public. Ultimately, inevitably, and tragically, their choices find them out.

Like these celebrities, we're all vulnerable to making dumb decisions. We may not be famous and rich, but we're prone to similar temptations and distractions. We too attempt to hide the truth of who we are on the inside, but eventually the choices we make define our identity and reputation. Legendary basketball coach John Wooden once said, "There is a choice you have to make in everything you do. So keep in mind that in the end, the choice you make makes you."[14]

> "There is a choice you have to make in everything you do. So keep in mind that in the end, the choice you make makes you."

The choices we make determine where we end up in life. Our hundreds of choices each day may seem inconsequential, but they are all pieces in the mosaic of our lives. They all make a difference. The text message we send, the movie or television show we choose to watch, the decisions we make behind closed doors—all reveal our values and shape our character.

Rethink the choices you're making:

- What are ten choices—good and bad—you've made today?
- What do these decisions say about your character, who you really are?
- Which of your choices draw you closer to God or make you feel alienated from him?
- Which of your decisions bring you joy and peace? Which produce guilt and shame?

Our brains are the most sophisticated, advanced computers in the world. Nothing man has ever invented comes close. Every second, millions of electrical impulses are firing in our brains. For years, experiences and messages have programmed our minds to think a certain way, and these established thoughts form our normal pattern of behavior. But the great news of the Bible is that we aren't locked in to the old habits of thinking and acting. We can reprogram our minds, learn to rethink life, and make different choices.

But reprogramming our brains doesn't happen by magic, by the click of some buttons, and it doesn't occur by sitting in church an hour a week. Like installing a new software program on your computer and working out the bugs, we have to take bold action to install a new set of truths into our minds so we can use them to shape our choices. This new program is God's Word, the truth of the Bible, the gospel of grace with its power to transform even the most wayward heart.

> We have to take bold action to install a new set of truths into our mind so we can use them to shape our choices. This new program is God's Word.

When Paul wrote to his protégé Timothy about living for Christ, he reminded the young man of his spiritual heritage and the way God's truth shaped his life. Paul wrote, "But you must remain faithful to the things you have been taught. You know they are true, for you know you can trust those who taught you. You have been taught the holy Scriptures from childhood, and they have given you the wisdom to receive the salvation that comes by trusting in Christ Jesus. All Scripture is inspired by God and is useful to teach us what is true and to make us realize what is wrong in our lives. It corrects us when we are wrong and teaches us to do what is right. God uses it to prepare and equip his people to do every good work" (2 Timothy 3:14-17).

We have a choice every moment of every day to determine the content of our thoughts. It's important to guard our thoughts, because what is in us will flow through us. We can fill our minds with God's truth, inspiring songs, and messages of hope and challenge, or we can let them drift into self-absorbed ideas that make us think we deserve more than we have. We can nurse petty grievances until they become huge problems in relationships, and we can compare ourselves with others and feel superior or inferior to them.

> What is in us will flow through us

In this passage, Paul tells Timothy how God's word changes a human heart. First, it tells us what's true. That's no small deal! The enemy and advertising try to deceive us, so we need the truth to remind us what's really important in life. As we focus on truth, the light reveals areas of darkness—in our culture, in our choices, and in our hearts. It shows us where we're wrong, not so we can feel ashamed and beat ourselves up, but so we can repent and experience God's cleansing forgiveness, power, and direction. The truth of God points us down the narrow road, and as we walk with God, we develop new habits of the heart: we learn to love God more fully, serve him gladly, care for annoying people, and rest in his great grace. That's the advice Paul gave Timothy two millennia ago, and it's still good advice for us today.

In recent years it has become my (Rodney's) heart's desire to honor God with the choices I make. Because of dumb decisions and boneheaded mistakes I've made in the past, I've learned the value of living in the center of God's will for my life. Unfortunately, I've had to learn these lessons the hard way. Some people learn from reading the Bible, and others learn by watching the good and bad choices of others. Some of us, though, learn only from personal experience. However we gain wisdom, the important thing is to get it! Nothing can compare to choosing God's best over any substitute the world offers. The two can't be compared. The most effective way I've found to block out the tempting voice of the world and plainly hear the loving guidance of God is to fill my mind with the truth of God's Word.

God's truth gives us a new perspective about everything and everyone in our lives. To change the metaphor: when we reprogram our minds with the truth of the Bible, we're putting on a new pair of prescription glasses that enable us to see more clearly. Then we can evaluate and make better choices. Knowing God's Word is crucial if we want to experience all that God wants for us. His blessings flow out of our deepening understanding of his character and purposes, and we discover those truths in the pages of Scripture.

Jesus valued the Bible and treasured its message to him. When he began his public ministry, Jesus went away for forty days to fast and pray. While Jesus was hungry and in a very weakened physical condition, Satan tried to distract him, tempt him, and lead him away from launching God's mission to rescue the world from sin and death. Satan took Jesus to highest point of the temple in Jerusalem and tempted him, offering him power and an easy life by avoiding the cross. But Jesus responded to the challenge by quoting God's Word.

All of us have a standard, a filter grid, a benchmark to shape our choices. If we're followers of Christ, our standard is the truth of Scripture. God's Word is the authority on which we base every choice and decision in our lives. The Spirit of God uses the Word of God to transform our lives. King David wrote, "Teach me your ways, O Lord, that I may live according to your truth! Grant me purity of heart, so that I may honor you" (Psalm 86:11).

Our minds are like sponges. They soak up whatever they come in contact with: truth and deception, honor and shame, joy and despair. We may think that we have no control over what our minds soak up, but that's simply not true. It's our responsibility to determine what goes into these sponges. How can we tell what's already there? That's easy. Difficulties squeeze the sponges of our minds. What comes out in times of trouble is what we've been soaking up for years. How do we respond to disappointments? Do we lash out in anger, blame others for our troubles, and feel sorry for ourselves? Or do we patiently and persistently cling to God's greatness and grace because our minds have soaked up the truth of the Scriptures that God is supremely trustworthy —even when we don't see him or feel him?

> Difficulties squeeze the sponges of our minds. What comes out in times of trouble is what we've been soaking up for years

We may say we believe the Bible, but what is the highest standard that determines our choices each day? Are we listening to the whispers of Satan—that success, pleasure, and approval are what matter most—or are we actively reprogramming our minds according to the new software of biblical truth? We face choices every day: physical choices—how we treat and care for our bodies—financial decisions, moral judgments, relational choices, and spiritual decisions. If we listen to the world and bend our ear to the way the world thinks and lives, we'll follow the pattern of the world's values instead of God's. Over time, we become trapped by a myriad of wrong decisions that once seemed so right but that we now regret. But it's never too late to change!

We need to be alert, though, because Satan's temptations come at our weakest points. He tempted Jesus with food, pleasure, and power when he was famished and weak. He tempts us to compare ourselves with others, demand our own way, use people, and focus on our wants above all else. And it seems perfectly natural, because that's what we see all around us. As the accuser, Satan reminds us of our failures of the past—sometimes colossal failures that hurt the people we love. Some of us can't seem to get beyond the shame of those memories. Tryon Edward observed that our future choices go a long way toward overcoming the pain of the past and gradually rebuilding trust in broken and strained relationships. He noted, "Right actions in the future are the best apologies for bad actions in the past."[15]

> "Right actions in the future are the best apologies for bad actions in the past."

Filling our minds with God's truth puts us in a spiritually proactive position, rather than in a defensive, reactive mode. Ignoring or trivializing God's Word causes us to be powerless, with no sense of authority in our lives when we're confronted with temptation. Too often, we simply give in. Sometimes we know we should do something different, but we're confused and disoriented. This state doesn't last long, however, because we often relieve the stress by eventually giving in anyway. We remain conformers instead of becoming transformers.

Michelle and I visited some very dear friends in North Carolina for a few days. The four of us went on a two-and-a-half-mile hike in the beautiful Smoky Mountains. Climbing to an elevation of around five thousand feet, we hiked a narrow path—only three or four feet wide—the entire way up the mountain. As we were following this path, we experienced a sense of peace, tranquility, and wonder at the beauty around us. The environment of the trail stood in stark contrast to the noise of the busy highway only a few miles away.

That trail is similar to the narrow path of walking with God. No matter what's going on around us or how fast the world is moving, we can experience peace and tranquility because we're on the right path and following God's way. All the craziness hasn't gone away, but in the middle of it all we find the presence of God. How do we find this path? By following God's map for our lives, his Word, and by shaping our choices around his truth.

IS YOUR CHOICE BASED ON LOVE?

As John Donne wisely said, "No man [or woman] is an island." Every choice we make affects other

"No man (or woman) is an island." Every choice we make affects other people"

people. Are we aware of the impact we have on others? Do we even care? The decisions we make can be driven by self-interest ("What's in it for me?") or by genuine love for people.

Jesus' temptations didn't end when the forty days of fasting and prayer were over. He faced tough testing every day as he served his Father and touched people's lives. Some of the toughest times occurred when Jesus encountered religious leaders who bitterly opposed him. One day during a clash between Jesus and the Pharisees, the most strict and influential sect of Judaism at the time of Christ, Jesus was cornered by a group of these leaders who hated what he was teaching. One of them asked, "Teacher, which is the greatest commandment in the Law?"

Jesus replied, "'Love the Lord your God with all your heart and with all your soul and with all your mind.' This is the first and greatest commandment. And the second is like it: 'Love your neighbor as yourself.' All the Law and the Prophets hang on these two commandments" (Matthew 22:36-40 NIV).

In this tense encounter, Jesus could have taken the easy way out by going along with the beliefs of his day. He could have said, "You have added hundreds of laws to the ones found in the Bible. That's cool. They're yours now. Live by them." But Jesus never sold out when people questioned his faith. He based his life and message on the truth of God's Word. In this case, Jesus took a stand for what was true. More important than any of man's systems for organizing religion was God's absolute truth: First, we are to love him above all. And second, we are to love others as we love ourselves. As the love of God permeates our hearts, it flows out of us into the lives of others.

Rethink the way you experience and express God's love:

- Consider your choices of the past twenty-four hours. When have you been most aware of God's amazing love for you? How did it affect you?
- Which of your encounters with people reflected God's unconditional love and bold truth?
- What mental software is shaping your decisions: the world's values or God's Word? How can you tell?
- Would the people who know you best say you're selfish or selfless? Would you agree with them? Why or why not?

Jesus was the least selfish person who ever lived. He based his life and ministry on selflessly demonstrating God's love to the world—even when his choices led him to the cross. As we face the myriad of choices and decisions each day, we need to ask ourselves the second question. Is this choice based on love? In other words, does the decision I'm making allow me to demonstrate my love for God and others, or is this decision motivated by self-love? Is it all about me?

Unless we've genuinely encountered the love of God and been transformed by it, we'll naturally use people and things to fill our hearts. But when the love of Jesus fills our hearts, then our desires, our relationships, and our choices overflow with the love of God. Paul described it this way: "Christ's love controls us. Since we believe that Christ died for all, we also believe that we have all died to our old life. He died for everyone so that those who receive his new life will no longer live for themselves. Instead, they will live for Christ, who died and was raised for them" (2 Corinthians 5:14-15).

Rodney and I (Michelle) are blessed to co-labor for Christ with a precious couple who have become our dear friends. We appreciate them so much because of the choices they made years ago when we first came to Orlando to start our church. They generously offered to open their home to host a vision night, where Rodney talked to twenty people about the dream for a church that would focus on reaching out to people who were far from God.

This couple, Steve and Deborah, were completely committed to their own church at the time. They had invested years of hard work there and had given generously to support the church that was sponsoring our church plant. They had also given their time and money to support the Christian school connected to the church. In fact, it had since become one of the top schools in the nation. Their children and grandchildren attended the school.

Steve and Deborah's best friends were part of the mother church. In spite of all of this, as Deborah listened to Rodney share the vision of Fellowship Church Orlando, God began to tug at her heart.

At first, Deborah was resistant to God's leading. She responded, "Oh, no, God. I can't have a pastor young enough to be my son! I can't leave our friends and the comfortable situation in our church to be part of a new church being planted. That's too hard." However, with Christ-like selflessness, Steve and Deborah followed the leading of God. They helped us build a church from scratch. Over the years, they've seen God use it to touch thousands of lives for Christ.

As I look back on our relationship with them and their contribution to our lives and ministry, I can say that we couldn't have done it without their wisdom, influence, prayers, and support. Their choice to join us made no sense to those around them, even their Christian friends and family. Thank God that they chose to do something different from the norm! And God has used them in a huge way. I'm so thankful for Steve and Deborah. They've encouraged me to take risks in making choices that may seem out-of-the-ordinary to do extraordinary things for God.

Love always leads to obedience. Christ taught his followers: "If you love me, obey my commandments" (John 14:15). When we're making decisions, we need to ask ourselves:

- Is this choice based on my love for God and the desire to live my life in obedience to the truth of his Word?
- Does this decision allow me to love God more and other people better, or is it all about me? Is it all about how it is going to benefit me—satisfying my needs, wants, desires, motives, and intentions?
- What choice reflects genuine love for God?
- Am I willing to obey, even if it's inconvenient?

Actually, our decisions are acts of worship. When we submit our body, mind, and will to him, we demonstrate that our love for God is greater than our love for ourselves. We are worshipping *him*, not our comfort or our reputations. In this way, our choices are the offerings we place at the feet of God. As we learn to rethink our choices, we ask: What gift have I given today to the God I love?

DOES YOUR CHOICE FULFILL GOD'S PURPOSE?

God sent Jesus into the world to fulfill a purpose bigger than we could have imagined. During the time Jesus walked on earth, he constantly faced difficulties that could have

---

107

distracted him from seeking, knowing, and fulfilling God's purpose. But he didn't lose sight of his mission. He was committed to doing the will of his Father and being obedient—even to his death.

One of the most important elements of learning to rethink life is our purpose. As human beings, we want all of life to center on our pleasure and glory, but God created us to enjoy the fullness of life only when we put him first. But putting him first is one of the hardest things most of us ever do! Everything in us wants to be on top, to be comfortable, and to win the applause of people around us. As the amazing grace of God gradually changes us from the inside out, we develop the most elusive and beautiful character quality known to man: humility.

> As the amazing grace of God gradually changes us from the inside out, we develop the most elusive and beautiful character quality known to man: humility.

Paul was a proud and ruthless man before he met Christ on the road to Damascus. When he writes about humility, we can sit up and pay attention, because he himself came a long way. In his letter to the Philippians, he encourages them to show humility instead of squabbling and bickering. Genuine humility, though, isn't something that happens naturally. It comes only from a rich, deep encounter with Christ and a grasp of the truth that he humbled himself for us. Paul wrote, "Do nothing out of selfish ambition or vain conceit, but in humility consider others better than yourselves. Each of you should look not only to your own interests but also to the interests of others. Your attitude should be the same as that of Christ Jesus: Who, being in very nature God did not consider equality with God something to be grasped, but made himself nothing, taking the very nature of a servant, being made in human likeness. And being found in appearance as a man, he humbled himself and became obedient to death—even death on a cross!" (Philippians 2:3-8 NIV).

As followers of the way of Christ, we need to stay focused. We need to imitate Christ's choice to live in humble submission to God, but first we need to be overwhelmed that his humility took him to the cross where he paid the ultimate price for us. Our humility flows only from the wonder of his selfless and magnificent gift to us.

Rethink your current focus and your grasp of humility:

- What are some signs that you're using people for your gain instead of truly loving them?
- What is your stated purpose in life? What do you want to achieve personally, relationally, professionally, and spiritually?
- What currently takes your focus away from this purpose? To what extent have you lost sight of God's purpose for your life?
- What does it mean to be truly humble? Whom do you know who is a good example for you to watch and emulate?

If we aren't careful, we can allow the world to distract us and get us offtrack from knowing and doing the will of God. Gradually we slip away, and after a while we find that we're no longer on-board with his agenda. We're back on the broad road that promises a lot but produces only heartache.

It's amazingly satisfying to look back on a particular time of life—a day, a week, a year, or a longer season—and know that we've given everything we've got for Christ and his honor. We certainly can't follow him perfectly; we won't be sinless until we see him face-to-face. But we can have the deep sense of satisfaction that we've wanted his glory over our own, have obeyed when it was hard and inconvenient, and have seen him work in difficult times.

Just before he died on the cross, Jesus uttered the words, "It is finished" (John 19:30). At that moment he was saying, "I've fulfilled everything that God sent me to do on this planet." We too need to be able to say that at the end of our lives. We need to live in such a way that others can see God in us and identify us as obedient, selfless followers of him. Our purpose in life should be obvious to people watching us, but ultimately it's not their approval we seek.

In the last week of his life, Jesus taught important principles of spiritual life. In one of his parables, he explained that there will come a day when each of us will give an account to Christ. Those who have invested their time and talents to honor God will see his smile and hear him say, "Well done, my good and faithful servant. You have been faithful in handling this small amount, so now I will give you many more responsibilities. Let's celebrate together!" (Matthew 25:21). That's what I want to hear on that day. How about you?

God doesn't want us to be like the iPod that stays hidden in a pocket. He wants us to shine like lights on a hillside for everyone to see. The choices we make aren't hidden. People are watching. If we choose to live for God, some of them will think we're odd, but many will be curious to know what makes us different. We need to live in the full light of God's love, with our good choices visible to everyone who is watching. In this way, we reflect God's light in a dark world, and our lives can shine boldly and radiantly for the world to see.

THE MOST IMPORTANT CHOICE

Before we go any further, we want to help you be sure you've made the most important choice in life: to enter a relationship with Jesus Christ. When we read Jesus' most famous parable about the prodigal son, we often overlook the other brother. He had been in his father's house, doing all the things he thought his father expected, but his heart was as far from his dad as his wayward brother's heart had been.

Studies show that up to half the people in churches every Sunday aren't sure they'll go to heaven when they die. That's sad and tragic! We *can* know. We *can* be sure. If our standing with God is based on how good we are, none of us can be certain of salvation. But if our relationship with God is based on his grace, on Jesus' payment of the price we could never pay, then we can be certain. In his letter, John wrote, "And this is what God has testified: He has given us eternal life, and this life is in his Son. Whoever has the Son has life; whoever does not have God's Son does not have life. I have written this to you who believe in the name of the Son of God, so that you may know you have eternal life" (1 John 5:11-13).

When we read the gospel accounts of the life of Jesus, we realize that there are actually two ways people can be lost. People can be far from God by turning their backs on him and willingly rejecting him, or they can be just as far from the heart of God by trying to prove that they've earned his acceptance. Within the first group of lost people were the prostitutes, tax gatherers, lepers, crippled, and blind people. Many of them realized their need for Jesus' love and forgiveness, and they flocked to him.

The other lost group included people like the Pharisees and Sadducees, the religious leaders who did all the right things for the wrong reasons. They attended worship services regularly, tithed, and followed all the commandments—but *not* out of deep gratitude for God's amazing love. They did all that to gain leverage with God and to feel superior to the people around them—especially the other lost people.

Jesus always spoke tenderly to the outcasts who came to him, but he reserved his fiercest words for the hardhearted, legalistic, self-righteous, proud, religious people. In his most famous parable, it was the elder brother (who represented the Pharisees and Sadducees) who stayed outside the feast because he was so angry that the father showed mercy to his younger brother. The message of the gospel—the wondrous forgiveness of God for anyone who is humble enough to admit the need for his grace—is available to every person on earth. Sadly, many people who are the most religious have hearts that are far from God.

Sometimes we ask people, "Are you a Christian?" or "Have you committed your life to Christ?" or "Are you a believer?" If they respond, "I hope so" or "I don't know," they're probably trusting in their own goodness—at least to some degree—to earn God's acceptance. But someone who trusts only in Christ's payment for sin responds, "Oh, yes! I don't deserve it, but God has forgiven me and accepted me as his very own. Isn't it amazing?"

So . . . what's your answer? Are you a Christian? Have you committed your life to Christ? Are you a genuine Christ-follower? If there's even a hint of doubt, take time to rethink your relationship with Christ. We want to share some truths to help you experience real LIFE.

THE LIFE YOU'VE ALWAYS WANTED
L = Love

God made us so he could love us and enjoy a relationship with us. His plan is for us to experience a full and meaningful life. God created us to ultimately spend "forever" with him. Jesus said, "I came so they can have real and eternal life, more and better life than they ever dreamed of" (John 10:10 MSG).

But if God created us to love him, then why do people feel disconnected from him?

I = Isolation

When God created us, he didn't program us to be robots that automatically love and obey him. He gave us a will and the freedom of choice. Unfortunately, we abused this freedom and chose to live apart from God. The result is sin, which causes isolation from God. Isaiah wrote, "It's your sins that have cut you off from God. Because of your sins, he has turned away and will not listen anymore" (Isaiah 59:2). And Paul explained, "For everyone has sinned; we all fall short of God's glorious standard" (Romans 3:23).

On our own, we can't attain the perfection needed to bridge the gap between God and us. Good deeds or religion or money or morality or philosophy won't do it. History is littered with personal, political, and philosophical attempts to reach God, but they've all failed. Solomon noted, "There is a path before each person that seems right, but it ends in death" (Proverbs 14:12).

So, what's the solution?

F = Forgiveness

Jesus Christ is the only answer to the isolation caused by sin. The Old Testament described a sacrificial system in which animals were killed to pay for a person's sins, but this pointed to the ultimate payment—when the Messiah, God's Son, would be sacrificed once and for all for the sins of the world. Christ's death on the cross paid the penalty for our sin and bridged the gap between God and us. He died on the cross and rose from the grave as a promise of new life.

Peter wrote, "Christ suffered for our sins once for all time. He never sinned, but He died for sinners to bring you safely home to God" (1 Peter 3:18). And Paul told Timothy, "God is on one side and all the people are on the other side, and Christ Jesus, himself man, is between them to bring them together" (1 Timothy 2:5). And he wrote to the Romans, "But God showed his great love for us by sending Christ to die for us while we were still sinners" (Romans 5:8).

When we accept Christ's death as the sacrifice for our sins, we are forgiven and accepted into his family. But that's not all. Someday we'll see him face to face.

E = Eternal Life

The death, burial, and resurrection of Jesus Christ made it possible for us to restore our broken relationship with God. We've been forgiven and adopted by God. The full and meaningful life God intended for us can become a reality, and we have the promise of spending eternity in heaven with him and his people. In the most quoted verse in the Bible, Jesus told us, "For God loved the world so much that he gave his one and only Son, so that everyone who believes in him will not perish but have eternal life" (John 3:16). And Paul explained, "The payment for sin is death, but the gift that God freely gives is everlasting life found in Christ Jesus our Lord" (Romans 6:23 GWT).

What an amazing offer! And it's free to every person on the planet. Is there any reason not to receive God's gift of forgiveness and cross over to God's side for the guarantee of eternal life?

LIFE MADE SIMPLE: THE ABC'S

At this point, some people may be confused about how to express their faith that Christ forgives them and gives them new life. Let's make it very clear—as simple as A-B-C.

A = Admit
We admit to God that we're sinners in need of a Savior.

B = Believe
We believe that Jesus died on the cross and rose again for the forgiveness of our sin and for our salvation.

C = Confess
We confess—both verbally and publicly—that Jesus is our personal Savior, and we make him the Lord of every area of our life. Paul told us, "Everyone who calls on the name of the Lord will be saved" (Romans 10:13).

There are many ways to express our faith in Christ. We want to give you a prayer that you can pray or adapt into your own words:

> Lord Jesus, I admit that I am a sinner and need
> your forgiveness. I believe that you died for my
> sins and rose again. I want to turn from my sins

115

and invite you to come into my heart and life.
I want to trust and follow you as the Lord and
Savior of my life. Thank you for saving my soul.
Amen.

Did you express this heart of faith to God? If you did, congratulations! You just made life's greatest decision.

ASSURANCE

The apostle John said that we can *know* that we have forgiveness and eternal life. How can we know for sure?

- Your assurance is based on the truth of God's Word.

Look at John's statement from another translation of the Bible: "This is the testimony in essence: God gave us eternal life; the life is in His Son. So, whoever has the Son, has life; whoever rejects the Son, rejects life. My purpose in writing is simply this: that you who believe in God's Son will know beyond the shadow of a doubt that you have eternal life, the reality and not the illusion" (1 John 5:11-13 MSG).

- Your assurance is based on the promises of God.

Jesus said, "I can guarantee this truth: Those who listen to what I say and believe in the one who sent me will have eternal life. They won't be judged because they have already passed from death to life" (John 5:24 GWT). Paul assures us, "For I am convinced that nothing can ever separate us from his love. Death can't, and life can't. The angels won't, and all the powers of

> A promise is only as reliable as the person who makes it. That is why the assurance of your salvation rest on God's character, not your efforts.

hell itself cannot keep God's love away. Our fears for today, our worries about tomorrow, or where we are—high above the sky, or in the deepest ocean—nothing will ever be able to separate us from the love of God demonstrated by our Lord Jesus Christ when he died for us" (Romans 8:38-39). And in John's gospel, Jesus promised, "My sheep recognize my voice. I know them, and they follow me. I give them real and eternal life. They are protected from the Destroyer for good. No one can steal them from out of my hand. The Father who put them under my care is so much greater than the Destroyer and Thief. No one could ever get them away from him. I and the Father are one heart and mind" (John 10:27-30 MSG).

- Your assurance is based on God's character.

A promise is only as reliable as the person who makes it. That is why the assurance of your salvation rests on God's character, not your efforts. The Bible teaches that God is faithful, trustworthy, and reliable, so you can trust his promises. Nothing will change his mind about your salvation, and nothing will separate you from his love. Your relationship to God through Jesus is secure. Paul told us, "God faithfully keeps his promises. He called you to be partners with his Son Jesus Christ our Lord" (1 Corinthians 1:9 GWT). And the writer to the Hebrews explained, "Let us hold tightly without wavering to the hope we affirm, for God can be trusted to keep His promise" (Hebrews 10:23).

- Your assurance is based on God's Holy Spirit who lives inside you.

To further guarantee your salvation, God has sent living, daily proof of your relationship with him. In ancient times, an official seal was placed on a contract as a guarantee. In the same way, God gave us the Holy Spirit as a guarantee of his promise to love, forgive, and accept us. Paul explained, "And because of what Christ did, all you others too, who heard the Good News about how to be saved, and trusted Christ, were marked as belonging to Christ by the Holy Spirit, who long ago had been promised to all of us Christians. His presence within us is God's guarantee that he really will give us all that he promised; and the Spirit's seal upon us means that God has already purchased us and that he guarantees to bring us to himself. This is just one more reason for us to praise our glorious God" (Ephesians 1:13-14).

The Holy Spirit at work within you is indisputable proof of your salvation. His presence inevitably brings changes. Some will be gradual; others will be instantaneous. The inward and outward changes in your life are the final proof of your salvation.

ONE MORE THING

If you've placed your trust in Jesus for salvation and understand that your relationship with him is secure and complete, you don't ever have to pray the prayer of salvation again. Your feelings may change, but your status with God is solid and secure. Your name is now written in heaven. Nothing and no one can take that away from you. But life has plenty of ups and downs. Being God's child doesn't protect us from trouble. Look at the life of Jesus. He trusted the Father completely and was totally devoted to the Father's will, and he experienced a lot of trials, including death! Don't panic when you face discouragement, doubt, and defeat. Giving your life to Christ is one of the easiest decisions you will ever make, but daily living for Jesus will be one of the most difficult things you'll ever do. Don't put your faith in your feelings, because they'll mislead you. Instead, put your faith in the facts and promises of God's Word.

Think about it . . .

Perspective

1. What were the consequences of a dumb decision you made? Did you learn anything from the experience? If so, what did you learn?

2. What's the problem with the following statements as they pertain to wise decision-making?

    - *Go with your heart.*
    - *Let your conscience be your guide.*
    - *If it feels right, do it.*
    - *If it's not hurting anyone else, go ahead.*
    - *What you do in the privacy of your own home is your own business.*

3. How can God's Word give us practical direction for daily decisions? What does it take on our part to understand it well enough so that it becomes the grid for our decisions?

Choices

4. Read 2 Timothy 3:16-17. Now read Romans 12:9-16 and apply the principles in Paul's letter to Timothy by asking:

- In the Romans passage, what is Paul teaching us?
- How do I fall short?
- What can I do to change so that my attitude and actions match the teaching?
- How can I make these changes into habits that last?

5. As you think about the things that have been most important to you, what choices do you need to make to live according to God's purpose for your life?

Impact

6. What are some specific ways you can allow the love of God to overflow into the lives of others? (Think especially of people you find it hard to love.)
7. What do you need to change so that at the end of your life God smiles at you and says, "Well done! You've done well, so let's celebrate!"

CHAPTER 6

ReThink Relationships

You don't have to be a "person of influence"
to be influential. In fact, the most influential
people in my life are probably not even aware
of the things they've taught me.
—Scott Adams

The cell phone in our pocket or purse can reveal a lot about us, and especially about who is important to us. Start with the screen saver. Whose picture pops up? What other pictures have we saved? When we scroll through the names and phone numbers in our contact list, we find our family and friends, those we call most often. Who's in our "Favorites," in our contact list, or on our speed dial as number one, number two, and number three? Someone could learn a lot about us by calling some of the people on our contact list and asking them specific questions about us. What would our family and friends say about us? (Maybe we'd rather not know!)

Then we can check out our Facebook page. What would our friends' comments on our "wall" say about us? If someone looked at all the photographs on our Facebook page, what would they reveal about what matters most to us? And how many friends do we have? And maybe more important, how many "friends" do we have that we really don't even know?

The people in our lives—our circle of friends, the people we love and respect, our favorite cell phone contacts, those whose photos are on our Facebook page—serve as mirrors of our souls. If we want to know who we really are, we can look at our friends. We reflect them, and they reflect us.

Our relationships determine the direction and quality of our lives. Without question, our close relationships with others have the single greatest influence on our lives.

As teenagers grow, their peer group takes on increasing importance in shaping their values and behavior. Studies show, however, that their relationship with their parents remains the most powerful connection in their lives until they leave for good. In their book, *Relationships*, Les and Leslie Parrot observe:

> Nothing reaches so deeply into the human personality, tugs so tightly, as relationships. Why? For one reason, it is only in the context of connection with others that our deepest needs can be met. Whether we like it or not, each of us has an unshakable dependence on others. It's what philosopher John Donne was getting at when he said so succinctly, "No man is an island." We need camaraderie, affection, love. These are not options in life, or sentimental trimmings; they are part of our species survival kit. We *need* to belong."[16]

In every stage of life, relationships can either make us or break us. I like how my friend Ed Young puts it. "We have to make the decision: are we going to invest our lives with the right 'they' or the wrong 'they'?" An important question we need to ask ourselves is this: What did "they"—speaking of our friends—influence us to do that we would not have done if "they" hadn't been around? Solomon wrote, "Walk with the wise, and become wise; associate with fools and get in trouble" (Proverbs 13:20). This verse has both a promise and a warning. If we walk with the wise, their perceptions about life and God will rub off on us, and we'll become wise. But if we choose to associate with fools, we'll soak up their distorted thinking, follow their destructive behavior, and get into all kinds of trouble. We have an important decision when it comes to spending our time with the right "they" and the wrong "they"; it's the choice between growing wiser or getting into trouble. We can't underestimate the power our friends have in our lives.

THE WRONG "THEY"

Choosing the wrong friends will take you farther than you want to go, will keep you longer than you want to stay, and will cost you more than you want to pay. When I (Rodney) was a seventeen-year-old high school student, I allowed the wrong people to influence me to make a dumb, what-was-I-thinking decision I've never forgotten. A friend and I were coming home from a basketball game one night. I was driving my father's sports car. We were cruising down the Interstate, when a pickup truck going at least ninety miles per hour flew past us as though we were sitting in a parking lot.

The young man who was driving the pickup had his girlfriend seated next to him. I could see her silhouette bouncing up and down as they flew down the highway. My friend—the wrong "they" in my life and in this story—said to me, "Rodney, are you going to let him do that? Come on, man. Let's go for it. Let's pass them!"

At that moment, I had a very important decision to make. I had to either say, "No, I'm not doing that," which was the wise decision, or listen to my friend and do something really dumb. You don't have to think hard to guess what I did. In a flash, I calculated the risks involved in both sides of the choice, and I determined that the biggest risk was to look like a coward in front of my friend. In an instant, I said, "Let's do it!"

I put the pedal to the metal and put Dad's sports car to the test. We went flying down the Interstate! Before I knew it, I blew past the pickup and left that guy in the dust. As I celebrated the moment with my friend, I looked in my rearview mirror and saw lights flashing. Not one but two state troopers pulled us all over—one for the pickup truck and the other for me.

When the trooper approached my car, he was ticked. He made me get out of the car and then put me through the whole routine—ordered me to put my hands on the top of the car, frisked me, looked through the car for drugs, searched his database to see if the car was stolen, and checked out my license. When it was all said and done, he showed me a lot of compassion. I was so thankful to him for that. Instead of writing me a ticket for going 140 (which is what his speedgun showed), he wrote me a ticket for only going 105 miles an hour.

My trouble, though, had just started. When I walked into the house and faced my parents, I got a lecture like I'd never heard before. To this day, I remember every word. Do you know why? Because I realized how dreadfully wrong I had been to listen to the advice of my friend. It took years of hard work—much labor, sweat, blood, and tears—for me to earn the trust of my parents again and deal with the consequences of my bonehead decision.

Rethink past decisions and how these have influenced your life:

- What is the worst decision you have made because you listened to the wrong "they"?
- How would your life be different today if you hadn't done what "they" encouraged you to do?

- How much guilt or shame have you endured because of giving in to the influence of foolish people?

Sadly, the negative impact of listening to foolish people isn't an isolated instance. When we spend time with people who aren't wise, we develop ingrained habits of distorted thinking, negative attitudes, and destructive behavior. Of course, our dumb choices are never *our* fault—at least, that's what we claim when things go south. From the time we're little kids, we learn to blame other people for our mistakes. We claim, "He made me do it." "She said it would be okay." "It's not my fault!" And even though we may find ourselves knee-deep in trouble for listening to them, we still crave the approval and acceptance from the wrong "they."

In fact, the more people get into trouble, the more they tend to avoid people who tell them the truth, and they hang out with people who tell them their destructive behavior is completely normal. Sooner or later, many people make enough bad choices that they crash and burn. This moment is excruciatingly painful, but it's God's wake-up call to rethink life and reorient their perceptions, values, and relationships. Some do so, but, sadly, some return to their foolish friends and self-destructive ways.

For us to overcome this harmful pattern, we need to be able to recognize when someone is the wrong "they" in our lives. Characteristics of foolish friends include these three:

- They live self-directed lives.

They only think about themselves, and they're only concerned about their own desires, interests, and demands. When they make decisions, they certainly aren't looking out for anyone else. Oh, they have friends, but these relationships always have strings attached. Such people know nothing of genuine love and unconditional acceptance. All of their relationships are games of manipulation. They've cut themselves off from the source of wisdom, love, and grace. They've chosen to run away from the will of God instead of living a Christ-directed life.

- They make poor decisions.

All of us have been around people who repeatedly make poor life choices. You'd think that after two or three—or two or three dozen—painful consequences, they'd learn their lesson, but they don't. They keep repeating the same pattern of behavior, suffering the consequences, blaming others for their problems, and doing it again. As a consequence, they carry a lot of emotional and relational baggage.

- They lack sound, wise, rational convictions.

We might think that foolish people don't know the difference between right and wrong, but that's not always the case. Many of them know very well what is the right course of action, but they choose to do what's wrong. Often, they have a deep disrespect for authority, and they demand to express their freedom from any controls or expectations. In every way, they want to avoid accountability and responsibility—at least in one or two areas. Quite often, they are so self-absorbed that they live only for the moment and try to have as much fun as possible—at anyone else's expense.

I've seen people go through all kinds of difficulties, but if they have wise and loving friends, they come out stronger than ever. But I've also seen people go through good times with foolish friends. Without exception, these situations were disastrous. Nothing has a more negative, destructive impact—spiritually, morally, financially, professionally, and relationally—than our hanging out with the wrong "they." Paul warned us, "Don't be fooled: bad company corrupts good character" (1 Corinthians 15:33).

Some naïve people think they'll be the only ones in history who can break this ironclad principle of relationships. They think they can spend all their time with foolish people, positively affecting them without being affected by them. The intentions may be noble, but the risk is far too great. Certainly we want to have a positive impact on people. Jesus was criticized for spending time with outcasts, pimps, prostitutes, and other people who had made a ton of foolish choices, but he didn't spend all of his time with them. It's perfectly fine—in fact, it's God's plan for us—to have meaningful relationships with people who have messed up their lives. The gospel reaches all of us!

But good intentions don't insulate us from foolish influences. If we're not careful, we have a greater chance of being negatively impacted by the wrong crowd than we do of making a positive impact on them. It is a lot harder for us to pull another person up than it is for them to pull us down. If we're not shrewd, we succumb to peer pressure, compromise our convictions, and conform to their ways. Instead of shaping their lives for good, we develop unhealthy relationships that destroy our lives.

> It is a lot harder for us to pull another person up than it is for them to pull us down.

THE RIGHT "THEY"

We long to belong, but we need a measure of wisdom to choose our friends. It's not always easy. Some of the most responsible, good, and godly people are quiet and unassuming. We might not even notice them at first. And we may have been in a crowd that makes fun of people who love God with all their hearts and have made lifestyle choices that are different from the crowd. How can we find wise people to shape and sharpen us? Let's look at a few desirable qualities these people possess.

* They're teachable.

We need to associate with people who have a teachable spirit. These people aren't puffed up with pride. Above all else, they desire to walk with God and do what's right. They listen to—in fact, they search for—sound advice. They become wise because they're sponges who soak in the wisdom learned by others. Solomon wrote, "Pride leads to conflict; those who take advice are wise" (Proverbs 13:10).

* They're humble.

Humility doesn't mean thinking less of yourself; it means thinking of yourself less. People who live in God's wisdom aren't self-deprecating, always criticizing themselves. That's not humility; it's a distorted, inverted form of pride. Humble people are so secure in the grace of God that they

> Humility doesn't mean thinking less of yourself; it means thinking of yourself less.

don't feel compelled to please others to win acceptance, to prove themselves by winning at all costs, or to hide to avoid being caught. They are thoroughly themselves, honest about their flaws and deeply grateful for God's grace. They walk humbly before God, and they also walk humbly before other people. Humble people aren't hard and inflexible, and they don't demand their own way. In fact, they have tender hearts. They love and respect others, because they model their lives after Christ. As the psalmist wrote, "[God] leads the humble in doing right, teaching them his way" (Psalm 25:9).

• They encourage others.

Foolish people are often cynical and negative, throwing others under the bus or stabbing them in the back, discarding people who aren't useful to them, and blasting people who get in their way. In contrast, wise, noble, kind people delight in speaking words of affirmation. They choose to fill others' emotional cups rather than drain them. They know how to tailor their conversation to meet the needs of people. They speak truth, but always with love. Wise people show the love of God to a needy, hurting world by speaking and doing good. Paul told the Ephesians, "Don't use foul or abusive language. Let everything you say be good and helpful, so that your words will be an encouragement to those who hear them" (Ephesians 4:29).

• They know how to forgive.

Real friends don't expect perfection, and they know how to handle situations when someone has hurt them. When they feel offended, they don't run away and hide, and they don't lash out in anger. They calmly and quietly choose to forgive the offense and talk to the offender about what happened. Even if the offending person won't admit he did anything wrong, the wise friend still chooses to forgive. Paul explained that we only can forgive to the extent that we experience God's forgiveness for our sins. We draw out of the deep well of experiencing

> We draw out of the deep well of experiencing his grace so we can forgive those who have hurt us

his grace so we can forgive those who have hurt us. He wrote, "Get rid of all bitterness, rage, anger, harsh words, and slander, as well as all types of evil behavior. Instead, be kind to each other, tenderhearted, forgiving one another, just as God through Christ has forgiven you" (Ephesians 4:31-32).

> Our relationships determine the direction and quality of our lives. Without question, our close relationships with others have the single greatest influence on our lives.

Lewis Smedes is an author and pastor who has written extensively about the importance of forgiving those who have hurt us. He wrote, "When we forgive evil we do not excuse it, we do not tolerate it, we do not smother it. We look the evil full in the face, call it what it is, let its horror shock and stun and enrage us, and only then do we forgive it."[17] He also explained that if we don't forgive, we instinctively seek revenge. Bitterness poisons our hearts and harms every relationship in our lives.

Smedes tells us what we can do about it. "Vengeance is having a videotape planted in your soul that cannot be turned off. It plays the painful scene over and over again inside your mind . . . And each time it plays you feel the clap of pain again . . . Forgiving turns off the videotape of pained memory. Forgiving sets you free."[18]

- They submit their lives to God and his will.

Wise friends have yielded their lives to God and continue to say to him, "Lord, I want you to have first place in every area of my life. It's no longer my will; it's your will. From this point forward, God, I'm going to follow you. I'm going to live according to your plans and your purposes." A right relationship with God (the vertical axis of their lives) gives them wisdom, love, and strength in all their relationships with people (the horizontal axis). They make a powerful impact on others as they live by faith. Paul explained, "The life you see me living is not 'mine,' but it is lived by faith in the Son of God, who loved me and gave himself for me" (Galatians 2:20 MSG).

Most people instinctively know who the right "they" are, but some of us are attracted to the wrong "they," because those people seem to live with such abandon and excitement. The cool crowd at school or work says to us, "We're going here. It's going to be a blast. Want to come with us?" They promise a fun-packed agenda, and we think, *It can't do any harm . . . just this once.* So we agree to go. After we have a blast hanging out with them, we put up all of our pictures on our Facebook page so we can tell the whole world, "Look where we were. Look who we were with. Look what we did. It was awesome!" But our reputation is ruined.

Rethink your relationships with wise and trustworthy friends:

- Which of your friends inspire you to love God and to love God's people?
- Who encourages you to make wise choices and live a life of purity and trust in God?
- Which of your friends accept you for who you are? Which ones accept you with strings attached and will ditch you if you don't comply with their requests?

Wise, loving friends accept us for who we are and support our life choices. They encourage us to do what's right, and they don't wink or laugh when we say we're going to cheat or lie. They're willing to say the hard truth to us when we need to hear it. These friends have our backs and want the best for us. They celebrate when we prioritize worship, studying God's Word, and serving the less fortunate. They don't criticize us because we refuse to compromise our faith to get ahead or be popular. They respect us, listen to us, and speak the truth to us, whether we like it or not.

For students, singles, and even married adults, our relationships should never lead us to compromise our purity. As believers, we are called to live a life of purity. This commitment isn't to earn God's acceptance; instead, our choice to say yes to God and no to sin reflects our grasp of his grace in our lives. John connected these dots for us when he wrote: "See how very much our Father loves us, for he calls us his children, and that is what we are! But the people who belong to this world don't recognize that we are God's children because they don't know him. Dear friends, we are already God's children, but he has not yet shown us what we will be like when Christ appears. But we do know that we will be like him, for we will see him as he really is. And all who have this eager expectation will keep themselves pure, just as he is pure" (1 John 3:1-3).

We want to honor the one who died for us by making wise choices in the places we go, the things we watch, the words we speak, the things we do, and the many other decisions we make. As we choose our friends, we need to ask ourselves, "Is this person inspiring me to make wise choices?" This is especially important in dating. Mr. or Ms. Right will never intentionally lead us into sin or cause us to compromise our Christian faith.

The primary factor that determines the direction and quality of our lives is our

> The primary factor that determines the direction and quality of our lives is our choice of friends.

choice of friends. We need to rethink our relationships so that we allow God to use the right people in his process of transforming our lives. If we allow others to control our thinking, we'll fall into the trap of the Evil One, who wants to steal, kill, and destroy all God wants for us.

BE THE RIGHT "THEY"

To build quality friendships, we not only *look for* the right person; we also have to *be* the right person. We have the choice—the privilege and responsibility—to become someone who builds good and noble people. It starts with our commitment to our relationship with God and the determination to be the person—the friend, the associate, the wife, the husband, the girlfriend, the boyfriend, the son or daughter—that God wants us to be. We have to accept the responsibility of controlling the spiritual climate of our relationships.

On a recent summer day, the air conditioner at our house went out. It was a blazing hot day. When the repairman looked at our unit, he said it wasn't going to be a quick and simple fix. We'd be without air conditioning for a while. Because of the heat, we were forced to move in with another family for a couple of days. We had to replace the whole unit, but they also installed a new thermostat. It glows in the dark, so I can actually go up to my thermostat at 2:00 in the morning and see exactly what the temperature is.

> Being the right person in a relationship means you are the thermostat; you set the spiritual or moral temperature in your life and relationships at any time, under all conditions—whether things are heating up or they're comfortable.

Being the right person in a relationship means you are the thermostat; you set the spiritual or moral temperature in your life and relationships at any time, under all conditions—whether things are heating up or they're comfortable. You don't just react to the current conditions of friendship, marriage, or work. You have your hand on the dial, and you take responsibility to set the climate of love, honesty, forgiveness, and progress. This is especially true for those of us who are parents—we set the thermostat of the home.

The Bible identifies a true friend as someone "who is as your own soul" (Deuteronomy 13:6 RSV). With this kind of impact on each other, it's crucial to choose people who share your beliefs and values. When you form deep emotional attachment to someone who is the right friend, God knits your souls together as members of his family. This kind of relationship is one of our Father's greatest gifts to his children. Scripture records a friendship like this. In fact, it's a picture of what genuine friendship can become. Samuel tells us about the relationship between King Saul's son and the next king, David. "The soul of Jonathan was knit to the soul of David, and Jonathan loved him as his own soul" (1 Samuel 18:1 RSV; cf. 20:17).

> For those of us who are parents—we set the thermostat of the home

After David killed Goliath, his friend Jonathan, Saul's oldest son and next-in-line to the throne, made a covenant with David to demonstrate his loyalty and love for him. Jonathan gave him his royal robe, armor, and weapons as gestures of that friendship (18:3-4). He was always humble, encouraging, unselfish, helpful, and fiercely loyal to David. But we need to understand what this commitment cost

Jonathan. He was to be the next king, but he was willing to give it up for David's sake. Even though Jonathan was the rightful heir, he remained a steadfast friend to David.

On a number of occasions, Jonathan put his own life at risk to protect David from Saul, who was trying to kill David and had asked Jonathan to help him do it. But Jonathan was loyal to his friend. He surrendered all claims to the throne and never took part in any of his father's attempts to kill David.

Jonathan and David remained friends through thick and thin. They pledged their love and loyalty to each other, and they also promised to protect and care for each other's families if either of them died (1 Samuel 20:11-16). When Jonathan and Saul died in battle, David kept his promise when he took Jonathan's crippled son Mephibosheth into the palace to care for him.

This friendship puts all other relationships in perspective. Jesus taught us about the true meaning of being a friend. "Jesus said, 'If any of you wants to be my follower, you must turn from your selfish ways, take up your cross daily, and follow me. If you try to hang on to your old life [perhaps those relationships: the wrong "they"], you will lose it. But if you give up your life for my sake, you will save it. What do you benefit if you gain the whole world but are yourself lost or destroyed?" (Luke 9:23-25 NLT, paraphrased).

What does it matter if you are the most popular, most well-liked person in all the world, but you forfeit your own soul by hanging out with the wrong crowd, spending time with the wrong "they"?

FRIENDSHIP AND PURPOSE

As we become wise and selective in our associations, we need to rethink our relationships and their effect on our life's purposes.

- Where do you want to be spiritually in the next twelve months? Which relationships enhance your growth? Which ones hinder that goal?

- How do you want to change so that you serve more gladly in the next year? Which relationships encourage you to give, love, and serve from a full heart? Which ones hinder this goal?

- Where do you want to be financially a year from now? Which relationships enhance good money decisions? Which ones lead you astray?

As we consider the impact of our friendships on our direction and purpose, we may need to make some difficult adjustments. Don't expect change to come easily! Changing our circle of friends inevitably comes at a cost. Our old friends wonder what's going on. Even if we try to maintain contact with them, they know they've lost their position at the top of our list of friends. And sometimes we make poor choices in selecting new friends. If we haven't been able to pick mature, good, and godly people before, we may find it difficult to know how to identify them.

Make decisions about relationships slowly. Don't jump in with both feet until you've had time to get to know people, to see them in different situations and find out if they are trustworthy. And as you move toward a new group of friends, you may find that your old habits die hard. It's easy to drift back into old attitudes, old behaviors—and then back to old friends. Then nothing changes. Don't settle for anything less than God's best for your life.

Not too long ago, as I (Rodney) was grilling on our back porch, I heard a very unusual sound. I opened the screen door and saw an owl in a big bush just outside. Immediately I ran inside and grabbed Michelle and the kids. I didn't want to scare the bird, so I whispered as loud as I could, "Y'all come out to see this . . . and be real quiet!"

When they joined me on the porch, I pointed to the owl in the bush, but none of them saw it. It was right there in front of them, but they couldn't see it. I pointed and described it until Michelle and the kids could see the big, beautiful bird. It had been in plain sight all along. We stood in silence and amazement. There's no telling how long this wonderful creature had been sitting quietly in the bush next to our door. We could have enjoyed it sooner if we had known where to look.

Owls are interesting creatures. In our part of the country, and especially in our neighborhood, they're rare, and they're difficult to see because they blend in with their natural habitat. Usually someone else has to point them out and say, "Look. There it is!" But when owls hoot, it's unmistakable. Their sound is a sure sign that one is nearby.

Wise people are like this owl. They usually blend in with the crowd. They may be still and quiet for a long time as they observe what is going on around them, but when they speak up, they stand out. Everyone knows they've heard the sound of true wisdom.

> Wise people are like an owl. They may be still and quiet as they observe what is going on around them, but when they speak up, they stand out.

The choice is ours. We can choose to walk with the wise and become friends with people who will enrich our lives. To attract these kinds of friends, we need to be careful how we live and make choices that reflect what the Lord would have us do. To *attract* the right friends, we have to first *become* the right friends. Paul told the Christians in Ephesus, "So be careful how you live. Don't live like fools, but like those who are wise. Make the most of every opportunity in these evil days. Don't act thoughtlessly, but understand what the Lord wants you to do" (Ephesians 5:15-17).

THE BEST FRIEND

What is the ultimate measure of friendship? On the night he was arrested, Jesus told his followers, "There is no greater love than to lay down one's life for one's friends. You are my friends if you do what I command. I no longer call you slaves, because a master doesn't confide in his slaves. Now you are my friends, since I have told you everything the Father told me" (John 15:13-15).

A few hours later, Jesus did exactly this for the people listening to him that night, and he did it for all of us who have been born since then. As the truest friend, Jesus willingly laid down his life for us so he could prove his commitment as friend, Lord, and Savior. Jesus Christ shed his blood for your sins and mine to rescue us from eternal judgment and bring us back into a relationship of love, forgiveness, and acceptance. It's what we've always longed for. It's what we were made for.

The grave didn't conquer Jesus. After he was pronounced dead by a Roman executioner, he was placed in a tomb, but three days later he came out fully alive. By coming back to life, he showed the world that he truly was the Son of God. Christ went through all of this so we could experience forgiveness and have the gift of eternal, everlasting life. Jesus did all this with no ulterior motive and no strings attached. He sacrificed himself out of pure love so that we could become friends with God. It may be hard to understand, but God loves you and me as his very own children. He created us so that he might enjoy us and be in a rich, strong, warm relationship with us. This truly is the greatest friendship of all!

How do we become Jesus' friends? We realize that his offer is a free gift. We can't earn it, and we certainly don't deserve it. He gives us his love in spite of our dark hearts, not because we've impressed him in any way. For this reason, we never have to wonder if we've done enough to earn his love; it is, has been, and always will be a free gift for us to cherish. Paul described it this way: "So now we can rejoice in our wonderful new relationship with God because our Lord Jesus Christ has made us friends of God" (Romans 5:11). Grace is the pavement on the narrow road God wants us to travel,

> Grace is the pavement on the narrow road God wants us to travel.

and we walk it with friends who are just as amazed by the unconditional love and forgiveness Christ has given us. There has never been a friend like Jesus. He is "closer than a brother," our closest and most patient companion, the one who never fails. The more we know him, the more we love him.

Think about it . . .

Perspective

1. Over the course of your life, who has been your best friend? What are the qualities in that person that have influenced you?
2. Read Proverbs 13:20. How have you seen this verse lived out in people's lives—both positively and negatively?
3. In your life, what are some results of having a strong relationship with a wise person? What are the results of being a friend with fools?
4. Who is having the most positive impact on you at this point in your life?

Choices

5. What kind of impact are you having on your friends and family? How can you tell?
6. Do you need to make any adjustments in your circle of friends? If so, what needs to change? How will you take these steps? What obstacles do you expect to experience when you take them?

Impact

7. What are some specific, practical things you can do to have a more positive influence on the people you love?
8. If your friends were to write something on your tombstone when you die, what do you hope they'll write?

CHAPTER 7

ReThink Generosity

"Pastor Rodney Gage preaches generosity
– and then practices it"
—Orlando Sentinel, front page
November 7, 2010

Prior to one of our church services, we secretly placed a plastic bag under each chair. I (Rodney) spoke that morning on generosity and the importance of stepping out of our comfort zone. I challenged everyone in the audience to take off their shoes and place them in the plastic bag—if they wanted to donate them to the local Rescue Mission. Within seconds, the atmosphere of the service radically changed. People looked at me like I had suddenly gone insane!

As I watched from the front, people all across the auditorium were taking off their shoes. Some were really excited; some looked more than a little confused. They'd never experienced anything like this before—especially in church! I told them, "Some of you will have to walk barefooted out on the parking lot. Some of you had lunch plans, and you're thinking to yourself, 'I can't go to the restaurant without shoes!'" Walking into a restaurant and letting people stare at them, I explained, might be the most powerful testimony they'd ever shared with anyone.

It was a moving experience to see hundreds of people leaving church and walking out to the parking lot toward their cars in bare feet, hose, and socks. Some of these people had come to church that morning with brand new shoes, and they were walking out without them. One lady donated a brand new pair of Prada shoes that cost several hundred dollars. To this day, our people still talk about this amazing, spontaneous act of generosity. It was a lesson of giving beyond our comfort zone, even when it doesn't make sense.

God is looking for open hearts that are willing to take steps to care for others. Generosity isn't drudgery; it's the most exciting part of our walk with Jesus. And when we step out in faith and obey him, God always blesses us in return. You can't out-give God. You can give without loving, but you can't love without giving. Giving is a natural by-product of our love for God and others. This is what rethinking generosity is all about.

Generosity isn't something we do; it's who we are. For the true follower of Jesus Christ, generosity is a way of life, a part of our spiritual DNA. Generosity doesn't start with our pocketbook. In fact, it doesn't start with us at all. It starts with God.

> Generosity isn't something we do; it's who we are. For the true follower of Jesus Christ, generosity is a way of life, a part of our spiritual DNA.

The message of the Bible is that God delights in giving good gifts to his people. He doesn't grimace when he gives to us, and he doesn't give it in small amounts. When Paul described God's generosity in the opening lines of his letter to the Ephesians, he said that giving to us gives God "great pleasure." He "pours it out on us," he is "rich in kindness," and he "showers his kindness on us" (Ephesians 1:5-8). That's an overflowing heart!

Do you and I see God this way? Some of us do: Our hearts are warm with gratitude and wonder. But some of us see God as angry and critical. We feel that we have to obey him—or else. Still others of us think of God as distant and aloof. We believe he's out there somewhere, but he's not really interested in what's going on in our lives, including our hopes, dreams, and needs.

The Scriptures tell us that God has an abundance of love for us. He is both incredibly powerful and tenderly loving. Most of us have a hard time putting those two traits together, but wonder and worship come from holding both in our hearts. The Bible says that God so loved that he gave. He gave his one and only Son to pay our sin debt. Because of God's great generosity, he gave us a clean start and new hope. He gave us forgiveness and a new beginning. He gave us a sense of purpose and a future worth living for. Through Jeremiah, God assures us, "'For I know the plans I have for you,' declares the Lord, 'plans to prosper you and not to harm you, plans to give you hope and a future'" (Jeremiah 29:11 NIV). We never have to wonder if God has a good plan for our lives. Even in times of darkness and confusion—and such times are part of every person's life—we can cling to the assurance that God is at work behind the scenes to accomplish far greater things than we can imagine.

Because generosity starts with God and is given as a gift to us from God, it will flow through us if God's Spirit lives inside us. But if the Spirit isn't in us, it can't flow through us. God doesn't expect perfection, but genuine progress is a sign of health and growth. If we're not changing, growing, and becoming a little more like Jesus, we may not really understand the depths of his love, grace, and power. But we don't need to wait until we find a huge cause where we can invest our resources. Instead, we can look around and find plenty of people to help nearby. [19]

Stop at this point and rethink:

- Is God's Spirit living and dwelling inside you? Are you being transformed—changed inside and out—by God? What are some evidences of this change?

147

- Is God's generosity evident in your life, your relationships, your financial decisions, and your giving to his church?
- Would others identify you as a generous person? If so, would they connect that generosity with God living in you?

For people who are consumed with God's grace, a heart of generosity is both a spontaneous overflow and a careful plan. Generous people think, rethink, strategize, and take action to be channels of God's love. It's a part of who they are, and it's a part of what they do. Even a person who used to be stingy and hardhearted can be melted by the grace of God and become generous. They are constantly thinking of ways they can give their lives away for the benefit of others and to honor God.

There is no single formula for what it means to be a generous person. People come up with all kinds of creative ways to give themselves away. They devote their time to help people in need, offer to pick up a child for church, help a neighbor with a project, give some of their favorite clothes away to someone who lost her job, pick up the paper for that elderly person and take it to the door, pay for the groceries of the person behind you in line, make a meal for a person who's sick or sad, have a new family in the neighborhood over for dinner, organize charities, serve at the church or other organizations, and use their financial resources to strengthen God's people and reach the lost. Sally Koch once said, "Great opportunities to help others seldom come, but small ones surround us daily."

> Great opportunities to help others seldom come, but small ones surround us daily.

God may not call us to give our lives away like Jesus did, and he may not ask us to die for our faith like some have done throughout history, but we have the power and potential to give our lives away every day to bless others. We don't give ourselves away out of guilt because we think we have to. Far from it. We give because we're compelled to let the love of God flow from us into the lives of those around us. If our motivation is guilt or comparison, we have some work to do to allow God's grace to sink more deeply into our souls.

Some of us have found a good rhythm in our generosity. We've loved, given, and served for a long time, and through trial and error we've discovered a pattern that seems right to us—and we love helping people! But others have gone to church for years, and they may have given money or time, but they secretly resented every dollar and minute they spent. And, of course, others are just starting down their road with Christ.

> We have the power and potential to give our lives away every day to bless others.

Sometimes, people simply need to know where to start. How do we go from selfish to selfless living? Making such a radical change isn't always easy. We may need to do some work on our motivations, and we may need to give some attention to planning. Either way, we should realize that there's a learning curve with generosity, just like there is with any other skill we're acquiring. Rethinking generosity is an important way to transform our lives and allow us to enjoy God's presence and purposes on earth. We start by taking one step at a time, but life transformation may happen more quickly than we ever imagined.

Generosity, though, isn't just about money. It's a product of rethinking what's most important in life and the extravagant generosity God has poured into us. When he captures our hearts, we gladly share our words, time, money, and message. And we're thrilled to see how God uses our generosity to change lives—including our own.

OUR WORDS

Generosity starts with our words. Generous people speak positive and affirming words of encouragement to others. Solomon reminds us that "an encouraging word cheers a person up" (Proverbs 12:25). We can be either bucket-fillers or bucket-drainers. We all carry around an emotional tank in our lives, and we can fill or deplete another's emotional tank by the words we say. Words have the power to build or destroy. We can bless people and help them reach their God-given potential with our encouragement, wisdom, and thoughtful words. There is nothing more powerful and potentially life transforming than our words.

> There is nothing more powerful and potentially life transforming than our words.

Our son Luke's ninth birthday was a great reminder of the power of generous words. We decided to celebrate the day at Disney World, where people celebrating their birthday get into the park free of charge. When we arrived, Luke signed in to get his free pass and receive a birthday button to wear that day. Disney also gave each family member a button that said, "We're celebrating Luke's birthday!"

As we went through security, all of the cast members greeted Luke and wished him a "Happy Birthday!" After we entered the park, people saw his button all day and wished him a great day. In fact, we couldn't walk ten feet without hearing, "Happy birthday, Luke! We are so excited to see you! Have a magical day!" All of the Disney cast members kept putting the spotlight on our nine-year-old boy to make him feel like he mattered. They were generous with their words, and they helped our family celebrate Luke's birthday.

This experience was a great lesson for our family. Throughout the day, I kept thinking about all the opportunities we have to speak affirming words everywhere we go in our daily routines. The people we see may not wear buttons identifying a significant time in their lives, but all of them need our kind and encouraging words. When we see people at work, in our neighborhood, throughout our community, on ball teams or the cheerleading squad, at school, in the workplace, and especially at home, we can learn to see them from God's point of view and realize that every person is a precious gift from God. They matter to him, and they matter to us.

Our words need to be full of respect. The things we say need to be words of affirmation, not condemnation. Scripture instructs us how to do this. We are to let "gracious words stream from [our] lips" (Psalm 45:2). A few years ago, many people wore bracelets that read "WWJD"—What Would Jesus Do? In the same way, we might ask, "What would Jesus say?" John tells us Jesus was "full of grace and truth." Are our words full of grace and truth, or are they full of manipulation, condemnation, criticism, and resentment? What difference would it make if we spoke the way Jesus did to the people around us—even for just a day to see what would happen? It would soon become a transforming habit that would have a powerful

> "Let everything you say be good and helpful, so that your words will be an encouragement to those who hear them"

impact on those we love, those we meet, and even on ourselves.

The psalmist said, "Gracious words stream from your lips" (Psalm 45:2). That's the overflow of a generous person's heart. They're gracious in the way they talk with other people, and they're devising strategic plans to have a powerful, positive impact through their words. Paul told us, "Let everything you say be good and helpful, so that your words will be an encouragement to those who hear them" (Ephesians 4:29). Imagine how our relationships would change if we followed Paul's directions!

OUR TIME

Generosity knows no bounds. As we begin practicing generosity with our words, we'll begin to look for other ways to let God's limitless generosity express itself through us. We'll want our lives to make a difference, and we'll use all of our resources, including our time.

We all have the same amount of time allotted to us each week: 10,080 minutes. No more, no less. We have the responsibility to choose how we spend those minutes. In reality, every passing minute is a moment we'll never get back. Without question, time is our most precious and elusive commodity.

Most of us protect our time very carefully. Even if we're wasting a lot of it, we want to be in control of our schedules. We want to have as much time as possible for ourselves. Most of us want to be able to maximize time so it brings us relaxation and pleasure. There's nothing wrong with that—unless that's all that matters to us.

But there's a lot more to life than pleasure and relaxation. God has put us here for a purpose. If we tap into his purpose, we feel energized, exhilarated, and driven (in a good way) to do more and be more than ever before. How do we give our time away—those precious 10,080 minutes in our week—to honor God and benefit others? How do we devise generous ways to maximize our time to partner with God to touch the lives of those who are in need?

We can begin by rethinking the connection between our purpose in life and the time God has given us. We might think, "There's a certain amount of minutes in my day today. I'm going to give at least some of these minutes away to bless this person, help this cause, and advance God's purposes in order to change these lives. I can do the one thing that I alone can do: Give my time away to other people."

Former UCLA head basketball coach John Wooden was one of the greatest basketball coaches of all time. He won an unprecedented ten NCAA national championships in a twelve-year period, including seven championships in a row with a record-breaking streak of eighty-eight consecutive games won. Throughout his remarkable career and the ninety-nine years of his life, Wooden was known for his inspirational quotes. A few of my favorites are:

"Winning takes talent: to repeat takes character."

"A coach is someone who can give correction without causing resentment."

"If you don't have time to do it right, when will you have time to do it over?"

"Failure is not fatal, but failure to change might be."

"Talent is God-given. Be humble. Fame is man-given. Be grateful. Conceit is self-given. Be careful."

Coach Wooden also told his players, "You can't live a perfect day

> "You can't live a perfect day without doing something for someone who will never be able to repay you."

without doing something for someone who will never be able to repay you."[20] He knew something about generosity.

God has given us only a certain amount of time to use (or waste). Coach Wooden's words cause many to reflect on how they invest their time each day, each week, for their whole lives. Take a few of your 10,080 weekly minutes to rethink how you use your time:

- How much of your time are you wasting? How much are you using on selfish purposes? How much are you investing in God by helping other people?
- Are you a slave to a schedule and never seem to have enough time? If so, why is that?
- How do you use your free time during the week and on the weekends? How do television, social media, or video games factor into your daily schedule? Do you need to make any adjustments?
- How do you want to invest time to have an impact on others? What could you do to make that happen now?

OUR MONEY

I (Rodney) still smile when I think about the Sunday I asked my congregation to stand and hold up their wallets and purses. I asked them to hold them high as I announced the title of the message for the day: "ReThink Generosity." As I looked out over the audience, I saw panic on the faces of quite a few people. Some of them looked as though they were going to have a heart attack! Everyone was afraid to look right or left, much less straight ahead, but I told them I wanted them to look at me. I asked them to listen carefully to me, because I wanted to make one statement extremely clear: *Generosity does not start with your wallet or purse; it starts in the heart.*

There was a huge sigh of relief as I told them to put away their wallets, checkbooks, and purses. I think I heard a number of them mutter, "Thank you, Lord," as they quickly took their seats. Others turned to their spouses and said, "I like this church. This is an awesome church. I am so glad I came today." It was hilarious to observe all this at the start of the message.

Money. Tithing. Giving. Stewardship. Generosity. In the hearts of many Christians, these are all dreaded topics. To be sure, they are challenging issues for most of us. We don't mind God giving us encouragement, and we love it when he provides for us when we have a need, but we get nervous when he says that he's Lord over our finances too.

That Sunday, I didn't want to run people off, but I also didn't want to leave them without a challenge from God's Word. As the saying goes, I wanted to "comfort the afflicted and afflict the comfortable." It's a delicate balance. As their pastor and leader, I wouldn't be doing what God has called me to do if I enabled them to worship the mighty dollar more than their Savior, and it would be wrong for me to focus more on the dollar sign than the cross. There's an order in God's redemption: When we experience a genuine, internal transformation by the grace of God, our external choices naturally change. True spiritual change always happens from the inside out.

Recently, life has been challenging for Michelle and me. We've had a lot of unforeseen problems occur with our home (such as our air conditioner going out) and kids (sickness), along with lots of inconveniences and disruptions in addition to normal craziness. About the time we were feeling most depleted, a wonderful, generous neighbor surprised Michelle and me one evening. She brought over a delicious meal to help us out. Our neighbor blessed us by giving away her time—by being generous with her minutes and hours to perform an act of kindness to let us know she cared. She was aware of the challenges we faced and wanted to help lighten our load. And she did that! Her compassionate act came at a very important time, but more importantly, she was blessed because she had the joy of being a blessing to us.

Our church started a ministry called People Care. With a church our size, I (Rodney) can't possibly touch each of these people's lives and meet their needs. Every week I feel overwhelmed by all the notes, e-mails, phone calls, and messages brought to our staff's attention about people in need. Some have been admitted or released from the hospital, are going through difficult times, are celebrating the birth of a baby, have had a death in their family, or are experiencing trials with their children. Their problems need attention, so we devised People Care to let them know they matter to God and to our church family. We encourage people to participate in this vital ministry by sharing their time, and the response has been heartwarming! With so many members helping out, we're able to maximize our time and efforts. Our people do what they do best: write notes of encouragement, visit people at the hospital, take meals to families, pray and send a prayer-gram, or provide some other needed service. There are countless ways our church family can spend their 10,080 weekly minutes to bless others in the name of Christ.

Generosity with our money flows out of our practice of using our words and our time to help others. Some needs require money as a resource to show we care. Some people get very nervous when a pastor or a writer talks about money, but when God touches a person's heart, he transforms every part of the person's life, including his choices about finances. The Scriptures tell us that a heart that overflows with God's love delights to give financially to God and his cause. We give cheerfully, generously, sacrificially, and intentionally.

One of the most touching scenes in the New Testament is when Jesus and his men watched as the offering was collected in the temple. They saw some rich people put in large amounts of money. Then a poor widow put in two small copper coins. Jesus explained the significance of this moment: "I assure you, this poor widow has given more than all the others have given. For they gave a tiny part of their surplus, but she, poor as she is, has given everything she has" (Mark 12:43-44 NLT). It's not the *portion* but the *proportion* and the heart that are important to God.

Too often, we have the idea that the money in our bank account is ours "because we've earned it," but God gave us everything, including the ability to earn a living. Once while I (Rodney) was opening our shower door, I noticed a large tree frog "stuck" on the glass door. Instantly I realized that this frog was an example of the way a lot of people view money and giving. As I looked carefully at the frog, I could see his sucker-feet stuck to the glass door. It reminded me of people who have sticky fingers when it comes to giving. Rather than letting go of their time, talent, and treasure to bless others, they try to "hang on" to what they have—and the cycle of blessing stops. We need to remember: the hole we give through is the hole we receive through.

> We need to remember: the hole we give through is the hole we receive through.

When a famine struck the churches in the first century, Paul saw the pressing, desperate needs in some of the congregations. The church in Corinth pledged to help those in need, but Paul wanted to be sure that they were giving out of full, thankful hearts. Grateful hearts are generous hearts; the two are inextricably connected. He wrote them, "Remember this—a farmer who plants only a few seeds will get a small crop. But the one who plants generously will get a generous crop. You must each decide in your heart how much to give. And don't give reluctantly or in response to pressure. For God loves a person who gives cheerfully" (2 Corinthians 9:6-7).

As an example to the Corinthians, Paul described the generosity of the churches not far from their city, the ones in Macedonia. They didn't give out of a surplus of funds. They gave till it hurt. Paul explained their motivation and actions.

> Now I want you to know, dear brothers and sisters, what God in his kindness has done through the churches in Macedonia. They are being tested by many troubles, and they are very poor. But they are also filled with abundant joy, which has overflowed in rich generosity. For I can testify that they gave not only what they could afford, but far more. And they did it of their own free will. They begged us again and again for the privilege of sharing in the gift for the believers in Jerusalem. They even did more than we had hoped, for their first action was to give themselves to the Lord and to us, just as God wanted them to do. (2 Corinthians 8:1-5)

If we only give out of our surplus, we're not living according to the generosity of God. Jesus gave, but not only when people applauded. He gave even when they despised him, tortured him, and killed him. Jesus criticized the Pharisees because their giving never affected their lifestyle, but he praised those whose generosity caused them to do with less for themselves. Paul described the hearts of the Macedonian Christians, saying that they weren't sacrificial because they felt guilty or pressured; rather, they gave themselves first to God, and then, as he thrilled them with his love, they couldn't help but give as much as they possibly could—and even more.

The last point in this section of Paul's letter to the Corinthians contains specific instruction about how they could give. He sent them his disciple Titus and another brother in Christ to collect the funds that would be sent to relieve the people suffering from famine. The Corinthians had made a commitment; now it was time to fulfill it. Paul encouraged them, saying, "Here is my advice: It would be good for you to finish what you started a year ago. Last year you were the first who wanted to give, and you were the first to begin doing it. Now you should finish what you started. Let the eagerness you showed in the beginning be matched now by your giving. Give in proportion to what you have. Whatever you give is acceptable if you give it eagerly. And give according to what you have, not what you don't have" (2 Corinthians 8:10-12).

The principles in Paul's letter apply just as strongly to us today. As the love of God changes us, fills us, and directs us, we love to give because we want to be more like Jesus. We give cheerfully, generously, sacrificially, and intentionally—and our giving makes a difference. God uses our gifts to touch many lives, and the act of giving puts us more in tune with God's generous heart. Isn't that what you want for your life? We do too.

Take a minute to rethink your giving habits.

- What is your motivation to give your time and resources to honor God and help others?
- Would you categorize your giving as generous or stingy? Explain your answer.
- What causes you to give cheerfully, generously, and sacrificially?
- What would it take for you to change your lifestyle and free up your financial resources so you could practice generous giving? Are you willing to do it? Why or why not?

When generosity is set free by a genuine experience of the grace of God, people get very creative in finding ways to help people. When our church had a series on "Crazy Love" and "Crazy Generosity," we gave our congregation five thousand dollars divided into envelopes containing ten dollars to two hundred dollars. We told them to respond to God's crazy love and use the money any way they wanted to use it. Instantly, the wheels started turning, and people thought of ways to help others. Some gave the money to help missionaries sent out by the church, but others used the money to help struggling single moms and young families so they could pay light bills or buy diapers for their kids. It caused our people to rethink their ability to meet the needs of people around them.

As far as I'm concerned, partnering financially with God is an absolute delight. That's the reason Michelle and I devised a strategic plan for giving generously. When we sit down to fill out our offering envelopes, we don't do it in a flippant manner. We don't imagine we're giving God a five-dollar tip as a thank-you for a job well done. We've prayerfully considered what we should give and how we can sacrificially make it happen. We plan our budget to enable us to give as much as possible. We adjust our lifestyle to turn loose of over ten percent of our income as our expression of love and gratitude to God.

When we give generously to God, we're saying, "God, if you gave away your life for me through your Son Jesus Christ, the least I can do is adjust my lifestyle a little bit so I can partner with you to help advance the gospel." Every time we generously give our money, we're partnering with God and saying, "God, I want to be your distribution agent. I want to get your message into the hearts of people. I want to spread your message as far and wide as I possibly can, so that every person hears the transforming message of Jesus Christ." If God's generosity is in us, it is going to flow through us.

OUR MESSAGE

As generosity flows from us, we realize that the message of God's grace is our greatest gift to share. The greatest gift in the world is the message of hope found in Jesus Christ, and he has commissioned us to tell people about him (Matthew 28:19-20). It's thrilling to share this message with people who have no hope. It's not our responsibility to make anyone believe. Our task—and our incredible privilege—is to tell them and let the Spirit work. When we speak the truth of the gospel to people, we take a risk, and sometimes we feel afraid, but it's worth any discomfort and any cost to see a person's eternal destiny changed. Paul told the Corinthians about this privilege:

> And all of this is a gift from God, who brought us back to himself through Christ. And God has given us this task of reconciling people to him.

> For God was in Christ, reconciling the world
> to himself, no longer counting people's sins
> against them. And he gave us this wonderful
> message of reconciliation. So we are Christ's
> ambassadors; God is making his appeal through
> us. We speak for Christ when we plead, "Come
> back to God!" For God made Christ, who never
> sinned, to be the offering for our sin, so that we
> could be made right with God through Christ.
> (2 Corinthians 5:18-21)

The spoken message is only powerful if we back it up with a life that represents the love and strength of God. He calls his followers to live his message. We have the privilege of generously sharing the gospel with the people God puts in our lives. Our relationships, and even our seemingly random encounters with people, aren't accidents of fate. God has put us right where he wants to use us. We begin with the people in our circle of influence—those in our workplace or at our school, our family, friends, and neighbors. God calls us to use our contacts and opportunities to be a difference-maker in people's lives. We can't afford to be selfish with the message of the good news. If we focus only on our convenience and comfort, we'll miss out on the greatest adventure of our lives.

Jesus made the choice crystal clear. Mark tells us, "Then, calling the crowd to join his disciples, he said, 'If any of you wants to be my follower, you must turn from your selfish ways, take up your cross, and follow me. If you try to hang on to your life, you will lose it. But if you give

> God calls us to use our contacts and opportunities to be a difference-maker in people's lives.

up your life for my sake and for the sake of the Good News, you will save it'" (Mark 8:34-35).

Rethink your generosity in sharing the message of Jesus Christ.

- Are you thrilled to be a child of God, to be forgiven and have eternal life? Why or why not?
- Are you hesitant or bold in telling others about your Christian experience and God's message of hope for their lives?
- Is your life message—the way you daily live your life—a good interpretation of Jesus' message to others?
- How could you improve in sharing the gospel message through your words and through your life? When will you implement these changes?

I (Rodney) had a conversation with a friend I had the joy of leading to the Lord a couple of years ago. I'm so proud of him because of the way he has grown spiritually. He and I met at Starbucks to discuss a sermon I'd given. A couple of weeks earlier, I'd spoken on generously sharing God's message with others. He'd felt burdened by my message, so he called me to talk about it. He said he felt that God was leading him to discuss his faith with one of his family members. He really wanted to do it, but he felt awkward and unsure. He was confused about how to begin such a conversation. He was concerned that his message might harm the relationship. He asked, "Rodney, is it the right thing for me to even consider doing this?"

My friend is a physician, so I asked, "If you had the cure for cancer, would you keep it to yourself, or would you give it to your patients?"

He replied, "Of course, I'd give it to my patients. I'd share it with everyone in the world!"

"Exactly," I said. "We have a cure for a disease far worse than cancer, and this cure is found in Jesus Christ. He shed his blood for your sins and for mine, and he gave away his life on a cross. He was crucified, buried, and raised back to life. He generously did this so we could experience forgiveness from all the guilt and shame of our past, present, and even future sins, and so we could have the hope of eternal life in heaven. All of that was given to us because Jesus gave his life away. And that's our message. The message that transformed *us* is the same one God wants us to use to transform *others*. As we freely and generously give that message, God will use it to change other people's lives. You and I are just the messengers. Jesus is the Message. We're to be willing to proclaim that message and generously live a Christ-like life before every person we know. If we don't tell them, they won't be told."

My friend knew what he needed to do. Together we discussed how he might share Christ with his cherished family member. We all can follow my friend's example. Each of us should pray and strategize with other believers about how we can be generous with our time, words, finances, and message, so that we eternally bless the people around us.

In our culture, being comfortable is a very high priority, but comfort is not at the top of God's list of priorities. There's a lot more to life than avoiding pain and finding as much pleasure as possible. God has given us a new identity and a new purpose. As we increasingly experience the depths of his love, our hearts will break over the things that break his heart, and we'll be excited about the things Jesus lived and died for. The pursuit of comfort leaves us shallow and empty, but a heart amazed at the love and power of Christ is willing to be what God wants us to be, to go where he wants us to go, and to do what he wants us to do. Then we don't have to *try* to be generous; it overflows from a full heart.

Think about it . . .

Perspective

1. Identify one of the most generous acts you have ever seen or experienced at the hands of another person. How did it make you feel?
2. Why is it crucial to see generosity as an overflow of our experience of God's grace? What happens when we forget this?
3. What might be some reasons generosity is difficult for many Christians? How does the culture cause us to be self-absorbed and protective instead of kind and openhearted?

Choices

4. Read Ephesians 4:29-30. How can you apply this passage in your conversations with people today? Who will you speak grace to? What will you say? How do you think the person will respond?
5. Time is our most precious commodity. How can you be more generous with your time and talents? What can you eliminate or reprioritize to free you up to give more of your time?
6. What would it look like for you to give your money cheerfully, generously, sacrificially, and intentionally?

Impact

7. How can you reorganize your time to know God more fully and fulfill his purpose for your life?
8. Who do you know who is generous with the message of the gospel? What kind of impact does that person have on others?
9. What is the most important lesson you've learned about the different ways to be generous? What stirs your heart to dive in to help others? What will you do now?

CHAPTER 8

ReThink Impact

You were made by God and for God, and until
you understand that, life will never make sense.
—Rick Warren

Since we moved to Orlando, our family has become a huge fan of the pro basketball team, the Orlando Magic. A few years ago during the first round of the playoffs, I (Rodney) took the family to see the Magic play. We purchased some tickets in the upper bowl of the arena. In fact, we were only four rows from the roof. When the game started, the place was electric. The fans were psyched that night. The public announcer would say things like: "Magic fans, get up on your feet and make some *noise!*" Then the fans would go wild! To fire up the crowd in our area, a man kept walking up and down the steps, chanting, "Let's go, Magic! Let's go Magic!" He was quite a cheerleader. Whatever he started in our part of the arena was soon chanted all over the building.

After he made several trips up and down the steps, some girls seated behind us became agitated and began to yell out obscenities, telling him to sit down. It didn't work. The more they tried to quiet him down, the more it fueled his passion, and the louder he cheered. The girls persisted with their cursing and obscenities, and it became very uncomfortable. I was far more disturbed by their actions than the exuberance of the self-appointed cheerleader. After taking all I could take from these girls, I turned around and gave one of the girls my "fatherly" look to let her know there were children nearby. When the girl saw me look at her, she said, "What are you looking at, you [expletive deleted]?"

I thought to myself, *I can't believe this. I'm just trying to enjoy a night out with the family, and I'm getting cussed out by some stranger who didn't like the fact that there were people excited about cheering for their team.*

The events of that night were an example of how our culture tries to suppress the voices of people who stand up and stand out for Christ. When we get excited about God and his purposes, we'll always encounter people who try to defuse our enthusiasm and destroy our message. It happened to Jesus; it will happen to us. When we face sarcasm, ridicule, or apathy because of our faith, we need to remember that Jesus stayed strong when he faced opposition. At one point, he was completely abandoned by those who had followed him. We may not face the same isolation, but if we stand up for him, we'll inevitably face ridicule. In those crucial moments, we need to realize that the important things in life always come at a cost. To stay strong, we have to be firm in our convictions. The old saying goes: "A person who won't stand for something will fall for anything."

During the basketball game, the Magic sometimes fell behind, and the crowd became discouraged and quiet. In those moments, the man in our area got up and yelled, "Magic fans, get up on your feet and make some *noise!*" Instantly, people in our part of the arena jumped up and cheered. Then the rest of the crowd joined in. Because one man led a cheer, the atmosphere of the entire arena was transformed.

One person can make an impact. One person who sells out to God can change the atmosphere of a marriage, a family, a workplace, or a school campus. Don't ever underestimate what God can do in and through us if we're willing to make some noise for him.

marriage, a family, a workplace, or a school campus. Don't ever underestimate what God can do in and through us if we're willing to make some noise for him. As followers of Jesus Christ, God has called us to be the light in a dark world. He wants us to make some noise with our lives by being different from the norm. He wants us to make an impact by changing the spiritual atmosphere of our culture. He has equipped us, transformed us, and qualified us to make a difference in the lives of people around us.

People are made to live for something—and Someone—far bigger than themselves. Instinctively, in the deepest recesses of our hearts, we know that God has made us for bigger things than the superficial promises of our culture. We want to make a difference. To make a difference in the lives of people, we need courage and determination. When we follow Jesus on the narrow road, we take the risk of standing up and standing out. This calling isn't just for missionaries and pastors. Every person who claims to know Jesus has the privilege of representing him to the people around us. There are no exceptions.

We live for a higher purpose with a deeper loyalty. We don't stand up and stand out for Christ because we think it's cool or we want to receive acclaim. When Jesus told his followers that he was going to be killed by evil men, they didn't understand. To Jesus, the sacrifice of the cross was the ultimate way of demonstrating the glory of God, but the disciples were looking for power and prestige. On the night he was betrayed, James and John asked for a favor: "When you sit on your glorious throne, we want to sit in places of honor next to you, one on your right and the other on your left" (Mark 10:37).

Jesus' answer was far different from what they expected: "You don't know what you are asking!" (Mark 10:38). He explained that following him would be a far bigger joy than they'd ever imagined, but it would challenge their socks off! God is looking for people who are willing to step out of their comfort zones and trust him to use them in big ways. Dwight L. Moody, one of the greatest spiritual leaders in the history of our country, was a man who was gripped with God's greatness and grace. He often told people, "It remains to be seen what God will do with a man who gives himself up wholly to him." He always quickly completed the thought by saying, "Well, I will be that man."

In a private conversation with R. A. Torrey, Moody remarked, "Torrey, if I believed that God wanted me to jump out of that window, I would jump."

Torrey later reflected, "I believe he would. If he thought God wanted him to do anything, he would do it. He belonged wholly, unreservedly, unqualifiedly, entirely to God."[21]

We need to rethink the impact God wants us to have on others. When we realize that God inspires our highest hopes and will use us in incredible ways, we dream about making a difference in the world around us.

THREE FRIENDS

In a dark time in Israel's history, the Babylonian army overran Israel, and thousands of her people were driven into exile to become slaves. In a foreign land, God gave a few young men the courage to stand up for him. Babylonian king Nebuchadnezzar built a huge statue of gold and ordered all the people of his kingdom to bow down to worship in front of it. But three Jewish men refused. When officials reported their defiance, the king was outraged. Daniel tells us, "Nebuchadnezzar said to them, 'Is it true, Shadrach, Meshach, and Abednego, that you refuse to serve my gods or to worship the gold statue I have set up? I will give you one more chance to bow down and worship the statue I have made when you hear the sound of the musical instruments. But if you refuse, you will be thrown immediately into the blazing furnace. And then what god will be able to rescue you from my power?'" (Daniel 3:14-15).

What would you have done in this situation? It would be simple to look for the easy way out! When we face difficult choices of integrity, we can think of a thousand reasons for giving in or getting away.

Students, what do you do when you go to a party and some of your friends offer you a drink and say, "We put a little something extra in there. Everybody's drinking it"? What do you do when all your friends are going to a dance, and the style of dancing is very sexual and sensual?

Men, what do you do when you're invited to go on a weekend fishing trip with the guys, and it turns into a lot of drinking, cursing, and coarse jokes?

Singles, what do you do when you're confronted with the culture that says you can have "sex without strings" and "relationships without rings"?

Parents, what do you do when your child wants to play a particular sport or activity, but you've previously said yes to several other activities that already compete with your spiritual, financial, and family priorities?

Women, what do you do when you're with a group of your friends and the conversation over lunch turns to poisonous gossip?

When we face these choices, we're in the middle of a spiritual furnace. Paul said our struggle isn't with flesh and blood, but "against evil rulers and authorities of the unseen world, against mighty powers in this dark world, and against evil spirits in the heavenly places" (Ephesians 6:12). It's a big deal. When we want our lives to count for Christ, we put a large target on our backs, and Satan tries to hit it with everything he's got! He'll use every trick in his book to discourage, distract, and derail us. Like Nebuchadnezzar, Satan wants us to bow to him—and to eventually give over the control of our lives to him. To stand strong during times of temptation and testing, we would be wise to follow the example of Daniel's three friends.

• Refuse to compromise.

The friends didn't run away or look for excuses. They looked at the situation, realized the great risk, and kept their composure. They told the king, "O Nebuchadnezzar, we do not need to defend ourselves before you. If we are thrown into the blazing furnace, the God whom we serve is able to save us. He will rescue us from your power, Your Majesty. But even if he doesn't, we want to make it clear to you, Your Majesty, that we will never serve your gods or worship the gold statue you have set up" (Daniel 3:16-18).

For us, the temptation to conform to our culture and take the broad road can come in large or small packages. Temptation may come when someone asks if we've said something about them, and we may try to lie to get out of it. When we're having financial difficulties, we may rationalize that it's fine to pad our expense report because a coworker regularly gets away with it. Similarly, we may reason that, since so many people gossip, it's perfectly acceptable to talk about people behind their backs. After all, we convince ourselves, they'll never know. And pornography is one of the most common problems among men. Some people call it "the victimless sin," but that's a lie. The person watching the images becomes emotionally detached from real people, his spiritual life deteriorates, and he rationalizes to the point that he no longer can tell right from wrong. But don't misunderstand: pornography isn't only a problem for men. Increasingly, women are getting hooked into "false intimacy" too.

We shouldn't be surprised when the temptations to compromise surface in our lives. It's part of the world's way of living, and until we die or Jesus returns, we'll face these situations. We first need to call them what they are, stop minimizing the situations or denying they exist, and draw a line in the sand.

There are many motivations to stand strong. One is that Jesus stood strong for us. In the hours before his trials and crucifixion, while he prayed in a garden called Gethsemane, Jesus wanted to bail out. In agony, he prayed, "Let this cup of the righteous wrath of God pass from me!" However, he didn't run away. He fell before the presence of Almighty God and prayed, "Not my will but yours, Father." Another encouragement to stand strong is the awareness that we live every second in the presence of God. He knows what's going on in our lives. He's not only watching, but he's also rooting for us to make good and noble choices.

- Rely on God's strength.

We exist in the constant presence of God, and we have access to the constant power of God. When we become Christians, the Holy Spirit takes up residence in us. He guides us and empowers us to live for Christ. We may not always sense his presence and strength, but even in our darkest moments, he's there. Paul prayed for the Ephesians, "May you experience the love of Christ, though it is too great to understand

> We may not always sense his presence and strength, but even in our darkest moments, he's there.

fully. Then you will be made complete with all the fullness of life and power that comes from God. Now all glory to God, who is able, through his mighty power at work within us, to accomplish infinitely more than we might ask or think. Glory to him in the church and in Christ Jesus through all generations forever and ever! Amen" (Ephesians 3:19-21).

Daniel's three friends also trusted in the power of God in their time of trouble. God didn't prevent the difficulty they were in. In fact, their loyalty to God *caused* their problems! Daniel explains what happened when the friends refused to cave in.

"Then [the king] ordered some of the strongest men of his army to bind Shadrach, Meshach, and Abednego and throw them into the blazing furnace. So they tied them up and threw them into the furnace, fully dressed in their pants, turbans, robes, and other garments. And because the king, in his anger, had demanded such a hot fire in the furnace, the flames killed the soldiers as they threw the three men in. So Shadrach, Meshach, and Abednego, securely tied, fell into the roaring flames" (Daniel 3:20-23).

When we're committed to standing up and standing out for Christ, we'll be thrown into the fire of opposition and criticism. It's inevitable. When this happens, we shouldn't be shocked, but sometimes it comes from a surprising source. Who were the ones who viciously condemned Jesus? They weren't the Roman conquerors. Every reference to Roman officers in the Gospels describes their faith. They weren't the foreigners,

> When we're committed to standing up and standing out for Christ, we'll be thrown into the fire of opposition and criticism. It's inevitable.

prostitutes, or hated tax collectors. They flocked to Jesus and loved him.

The religious leaders felt threatened by Jesus, so they were the ones who mocked him, criticized him, and eventually turned him over to be tortured and killed. We shouldn't be surprised if some church people feel very uncomfortable with our zeal to live wholeheartedly for Jesus. They often have their neat, tidy way of orchestrating spiritual life with little room for passionate devotion. It's sad but too often true. Of course, there may be some unbelievers who are very critical of the Christian faith, while others admire believers for standing up for what they believe. Read the Gospels and Acts to see who opposed Jesus, Peter, and Paul. It's not a big jump to imagine who may oppose us as we stand up for Christ.

• Remember God's presence.

If people are vicious and attack you for your beliefs, and you have prayed for deliverance but it hasn't come, don't give up. God's deliverance comes in many different forms. The early Christians endured severe persecution, but God used their steadfast faith when they were tortured as "seeds" that produced an incredible harvest of new believers. God's purposes aren't always to protect us from harm or quickly get us out of problems. He will strengthen us, even in the middle of our greatest difficulties. And, yes, sometimes God does the miraculous to rescue us.

When the three young men were thrown into the roaring flames, they were willing to accept God's will, even if it meant death. God's plan—for those men, at that time, for his purposes—was to deliver them in a way that caused the most powerful king on earth to sit up and take notice. Daniel describes the scene.

But suddenly, Nebuchadnezzar jumped up in amazement and exclaimed to his advisers, "Didn't we tie up three men and throw them into the furnace?" "Yes, Your Majesty, we certainly did," they replied. "Look!" Nebuchadnezzar shouted. "I see four men, unbound, walking around in the fire unharmed! And the fourth looks like a god!" Then Nebuchadnezzar came as close as he could to the door of the flaming furnace and shouted: "Shadrach, Meshach, and Abednego, servants of the Most High God, come out! Come here!" So Shadrach, Meshach, and Abednego stepped out of the fire. Then the high officers, officials, governors, and advisers crowded around them and saw that the fire had not touched them. Not a hair on their heads was singed, and their clothing was not scorched. They didn't even smell of smoke! (Daniel 3:24-27)

About two hundred years later, God spoke a similar message through the prophet Isaiah to encourage people who had lost hope in God's presence, power, and purpose: "When you go through deep waters, I will be with you. When you go through rivers of difficulty, you will not drown. When you walk through the fire of oppression, you will not be burned up; the flames will not consume you. For I am the Lord, your God" (Isaiah 43:2-3).

We often want guarantees that God will show up *when* we want him to, *how* we want him to, and to do *what* we expect him to—but our comfort and safety aren't his highest priorities. The guarantee we can count on is that God is the sovereign ruler of the universe, and his plans are good and right. We can trust him—not because we know what he's up to and approve of his plans, but because he has proven he is supremely worthy of our deepest trust and love. The pages of Scripture and history show us that God's plans are often very different than what we'd expect or desire. Walking with him often means trusting him when we hit dead-ends.

- Receive God's promotion.

Glory isn't some strange, abstract concept. The word itself means "affirmation, especially by an authority higher and greater than ourselves." Jesus glorified the Father by pointing out his transcendent love and majesty. We glorify God every time we reflect a bit of his kindness, strength, and purposes. It's important to note that we aren't always on the giving end of glory. We also receive glory from God as we trust him. When Jesus was baptized, and also when he was transfigured on the mountain, the Father spoke out of heaven with words of strong and tender affirmation. As his children, we hear God speak to our hearts too: "You are my beloved son or daughter in whom I'm well pleased!" And when we use our talents and resources to honor him, he tells us, "Well done! Let's celebrate your faithfulness!"

When the three friends were rescued out of the fire by the fourth person (which was an appearance of Christ called a *Christophany*), Daniel tells us what happened next.

> Then Nebuchadnezzar said, "Praise to the God of Shadrach, Meshach, and Abednego! He sent his angel to rescue his servants who trusted in him. They defied the king's command and were willing to die rather than serve or worship any god except their own God. Therefore, I make this decree: If any people, whatever their race

> or nation or language, speak a word against the
> God of Shadrach, Meshach, and Abednego,
> they will be torn limb from limb, and their
> houses will be turned into heaps of rubble.
> There is no other god who can rescue like this!"
> Then the king promoted Shadrach, Meshach,
> and Abednego to even higher positions in the
> province of Babylon. (Daniel 3:28-30)

We may never hear such words from earthly authorities, but we'll certainly hear them from Almighty God, the King of all kings. He delights in our love and cherishes our courage to stand up for him. People around us may have varied responses to our devotion to our Lord. They may applaud—or snarl and walk away. They responded that way to Jesus. We shouldn't expect anything different.

We live in an instant society, and we expect God to answer our prayers on our do-it-now timetable. One of our greatest temptations is to bail out before the breakthrough comes. Waiting on God is essential if we are going to be the people he wants us to be. It is the height of arrogance to think we know better than God how things should go. Instead of demanding

> One of our greatest temptations is to bail before the breakthrough comes.

our way and our timing, we should humbly acknowledge that he "holds all things in the hollow of his hand." We can trust him. He will never fail us.

ON THE ROAD

It's deceptively easy to miss something that's right in front of us. When Jesus explained that God's ultimate desire for us is to love him with all our hearts and let that love overflow in our love for others, a man asked, "Who is my neighbor?" While the man felt comfortable caring for people who were just like him (and who may not have needed much help), he was challenged when Jesus told him a story about loving a despised outcast.

In those days, Samaritans were at the bottom of the barrel in Palestinian culture. The Jews went to great lengths to avoid any contact with them. In Jesus' story, a man had been on a journey from Jerusalem to Jericho. It was a dangerous route because bandits often attacked people on that road. Two religious people came upon the traveler, who was beaten and bleeding, lying in the dirt. Because they didn't want to get their hands dirty, they walked on by. A Samaritan also traveled the road that day. When he saw the man on the ground, his heart was touched. He bandaged his wounds and carried him on his donkey to a nearby inn. Once there, the Samaritan paid for the man's lodging and care.

The point of the story is that we all need to rethink the kind of impact God wants us to have. If we protect ourselves from every inconvenience, we won't be open to touching the lives of needy people around us. The two religious people were on the road and saw the man's need, but they found excuses to avoid getting involved. Loving people always comes with a price tag—in time and energy—but not helping them carries the much higher cost of a cold heart.

> You're the light of the world, so shine! You're the salt of the earth. Be tasty and attractive! Rethink the kind of impact God wants you to have in the lives of the people you see each day.

Always value love over comfort. Get involved. You don't have to go to Africa to find needs and meet them. Hurting, lonely, desperate people are all around you—maybe even under your roof. You're the light of the world, so shine! You're the salt of the earth. Be tasty and attractive! Rethink the kind of impact God wants you to have in the lives of the people you see each day. Then give everything you've got to show his love to them.

STANDING UP, STANDING OUT

When Welles Crowther was eight years old, his father gave him a red bandanna. He told his son to carry it with him always because it would make him stand out. He wore it around the house, in school, and under his lacrosse helmet when he played for Boston College. After he graduated, he became an equities trader in New York. His office was on the 104th floor of the South Tower of the World Trade Center.

When the planes hit on the morning of September 11, 2001, many people panicked in the chaos of flames, debris, collapsed ceilings, confusion, death, and blocked stairwells. But not Welles. Eyewitnesses who escaped from the upper stories of the South Tower talked about a man wearing a red bandanna who led countless people down twenty flights of stairs to safety. He carried a woman on his back down fifteen flights. Because of his courage and compassion, they made it to safety, but he always went back up to find more people.

For over an hour, he labored to rescue as many as possible. Then the tower came down. Later, those he helped talked about a man in a red bandanna. They didn't know his name, his office, or his title, but they all remarked that he wore a bandanna over his nose and mouth to keep from suffocating in the smoke and ash. And he saved their lives.

Welles' father was right. The bandanna would cause him to stand out in a crowd someday. The piece of cloth was a symbol of his father's vision for his life's purpose. When people needed help, Welles was ready. He fulfilled his destiny.

Our Father has given us a bold, inspiring vision for our life's purpose. We can make a difference in the lives of people around us. We just need to be ready.

> We can make a difference in the lives of people around us. We just need to be ready.

If you've read to the end of this book, you've shown that you're genuinely interested in being on the narrow road with Jesus. That's fantastic! We applaud your tender heart and courage to take bold steps with Christ with us. Don't stop now. If you've been on that road for decades, or if you've just taken a few initial steps, there's a lot to learn. Every step is an adventure that challenges you to the core and inspires you to live life at a whole new level. Hold his hand and hang on! The best is yet to come!

Think about it . . .

Perspective

1. Have you ever seen one person's enthusiasm and boldness change the mood of a large group? What happened?
2. What are good motivations to stand up and stand out for Christ? What are some motives that aren't so good? How can you tell the difference?

3. What part of the story of Daniel's three friends encourages you the most? What part scares you?

Choices

4. What are some common temptations and tests people face? What are some that you face? How are you handling them?
5. How can remembering God's strength and his presence give you courage to stand strong?
6. Why is it so hard to wait? What does our impatience say about our perspective of God's wisdom and will? What are some truths that will help you wait on God?

Impact

7. Where has God put you to shine as a light for him? Who are the people he has put on your heart?
8. What do you need to be and do to be a good partner in God's enterprise?
9. What's the most important truth or principle you'll take away from this book? How has God used it in your life? How do you want him to use it to change you, direct you, and inspire you?

USING *RETHINK* LIFE IN CLASSES AND GROUPS

This book is designed for individual study, small groups, and classes. The best way to absorb and apply these principles is for each person to individually study and answer the questions at the end of each chapter and then discuss them in either a class or a group environment.

Each chapter's questions are designed to promote reflection, application, and discussion. Order enough copies of the book for everyone to have a copy. Encourage couples to have a book for each of them so they can record their individual reflections.

A recommended schedule for a small group or class might be:

Week 1: Introduce the material. As a group leader, tell your story of finding and fulfilling the dream God has given you, share your hopes for the group, and provide a book for each person. Encourage people to read the assigned chapter each week and answer the questions.

Weeks 2-9: Each week, introduce the topic for the week and share a story of how God has used the principles in your life. In small groups, lead people through a discussion of the questions at the end of the chapter. In classes, teach the principles in each chapter, use personal illustrations, and invite discussion.

PERSONALIZE EACH LESSON

Don't feel pressured to cover every question in your group discussions. Pick out three or four that had the biggest impact on you, and focus on those, or ask people in the group to share their responses to the questions that meant the most to them that week.

Make sure you personalize the principles and applications. At least once in each group meeting, add your own story to illustrate a particular point.

Make the Scriptures come alive. Far too often, we read the Bible like it's a phone book, with little or no emotion. Paint a vivid picture for people. Provide insights about the context of people's encounters with God, and help people in your class or group sense the emotions of specific people in each scene.

FOCUS ON APPLICATION

The questions at the end of each chapter—and your encouragement to group members to be authentic—will help your group take big steps to apply the principles they're learning. Share how you are applying the principles from particular chapters each week, and encourage them to take steps of growth too.

THREE TYPES OF QUESTIONS

If you have led groups for a few years, you already understand the importance of using open questions to stimulate discussion. There are three types of questions: *limiting, leading,* and *open.* Many of the questions at the end of each lesson are *open* questions.

Limiting questions focus on an obvious answer, such as, "What does Jesus call himself in John 10:11?" These don't stimulate reflection or discussion. If you want to use questions like this, follow them with thought-provoking, open questions.

Leading questions require the listener to guess what the leader has in mind, such as, "Why did Jesus use the metaphor of a shepherd in John 10?" (He was probably alluding to a passage in Ezekiel, but many people don't know that.) The teacher who asks a leading question has a definite answer in mind. Instead of asking this kind of question, you should just teach the point and then perhaps ask an open question about the point you made.

Open questions usually don't have right or wrong answers. They stimulate thinking, and they are far less threatening than other kinds of questions because the person answering doesn't risk ridicule for being wrong. These questions often begin with "Why do you think . . . ?" or "What are some reasons that . . . ?" or "How would you have felt in that situation?"

PREPARATION

As you prepare to teach this material in a group or class, consider these steps:

1. Carefully and thoughtfully read the book. Make notes; highlight key sections, quotes, or stories; and complete the reflection section at the end of each chapter. This will familiarize you with the entire scope of the content.
2. As you prepare for each week's class or group, read the corresponding chapter again and make additional notes.

3. Tailor the amount of content to the time allotted. You won't have time to cover all the questions, so pick the ones that are most pertinent.
4. Add your own stories to personalize the message and add impact.
5. Before and during your preparation, ask God to give you wisdom, clarity, and power. Trust him to use your group to change people's lives.
6. Most people will get far more out of the group if they read the chapter and complete the reflection each week. Order books before the group or class begins or after the first week.

NOTES

1   Cited by Jason Harvey in *Achieving Anything in Just One Year* (Amazing Life Press, 2010), 1.

2   Os Guinness, *The Call: Finding and Fulfilling the Central Purpose of Your Life* (Nashville: Thomas Nelson, 2003), 4.

3   Søren Kierkegaard, *The Prayers of Kierkegaard*, ed. Perry LeFebre (Chicago: University of Chicago, 1956), 147.

4   Scott Peck, *The Road Less Traveled* (New York: Simon & Schuster, 1978), 15.

5   Cited by Roy B. Zuck, *The Speaker's Quote Book* (Kregel Academic & Professional, 1997), 387.

6   Charles Swindoll, *Encouragement for Life* (Nashville: Thomas Nelson, 2006), 115.

7   Joyce Meyer, *The Power of Determination* (FaithWords, 2003).

8   Cited by Dave Browning in *Deliberate Simplicity* (Grand Rapids: Zondervan, 2009), 38.

9   Anne Ortlund, *Disciplines of the Beautiful Woman* (Waco, Texas: Word Books, 1977).

10 Leander Kahney, "Straight Dope on the iPod's Birth," October 17, 2006. *Wired News: www.wired.com*, (retrieved January 31, 2011).

11 Tom Hormby and Dan Knight, "A History of the iPod: 2000 to 2004," *Tom Hormby's Orchard*, lowendmac.com, 2005.10.14, retrieved 2011.01.31.

12 Katie Marsal, "iPod: how big can it get?" *AppleInsider*, appleinsider.com, 2006.05.24, retrieved 2011.01.31.

13 Cited by John C. Maxwell in *Leadership Gold*, (Thomas Nelson, 2008.

14 Cited by Eric Watterson in *The Path of Forgiveness Book 3*, (SON Enterprises, 2010), 5.

15 Drs. Les and Leslie Parrott, *Relationships*, (Zondervan, Grand Rapids, 1998), 11.

16 Lewis Smedes, *Forgive and Forget*, (Harper & Row, 1984), 79-80.

17 Lewis Smedes, cited in *Forgiving Others and Trusting God*, (Xulon Press, 2011), 32.

18 Cited by Anne Brentar in *Find the Key to Your Success*, (Xlibris, 2008), 18.

19 Quotes cited on CoachWooden.com.

20 R. A. Torrey, "Why God Used D. L. Moody," cited at www.wholesomewords.org/biography/biomoody6.html.

Other Books by Rodney Gage

We Can Work It Out
Creative Conflict Resolution with Your Teen
The Book offers profound insights into the cause and effect of parent/teen conflict, as well as creative, Christ-centered approaches to effective conflict resolution. Find hope and encouragement for lasting change-peace and harmony- in any home.

Why Your Kids Do What They Do
Responding To The Driving Forces Behind Your Teen's Behavior
Rodney Gage draws knowledge from the latest studies of how unmet needs are directly related to negative attitudes and behaviors. He has created a book that helps parents understand their teens, understand themselves, and learn to know and love one another.

Becoming The Parent Your Teenager Needs
Inspirations for Daily Encouragement
Just the book parents need during the most trying times of their lives-when their children become teenagers! Gage shows readers that they are not alone in their struggle to raise healthy, happy, well-adjusted young adults. Each inspiration ends with a Scripture quote, a daily challenge, a daily reflection, and a daily prayer.

If My Parents Knew...
Discovering Your Teenager's Unspoken Needs
If My Parents Knew...What I like about them, What I really need from them, How much I want to be somebody, How my friends make me feel, My fears and Questions about sex, and Much more. **If My Parents Knew...** offers common sense advice for parenting teenagers. This informative book contains letters Gage has received from teenagers across the nation revealing what they desire most in their relationships with their parents.

To purchase these books log onto www.rodneygage.com

Join the Movement

ReThink Life Experiment for Churches

40-Day Church-Wide Campaign
Resources Available Online:

www.ReThinkLife.com

www.fellowshiporlando.com
Facebook/Fellowship Orlando
Twitter/fochurch

Fellowship Orlando is a biblically driven church that offers
practical teaching in a relevant,
life-giving environment that is alive with energy and creativity.

Women's Conference

ReThink Pink is a movement of women who have decided not to conform to their culture, but are determined to change it. We do this by making the ReThink Pink principles a part of our everyday lives... Knowing your Purpose, Living God's Priorities, Choosing Purity & Sharing your Passion.

For more information or to register for the next
reThink Pink Conference
www.rethinkpinkconference.com
facebook.com/rethinkpink

CPSIA information can be obtained at www.ICGtesting.com
Printed in the USA
LVOW060219270712

291711LV00001B/4/P